When Owing a Shilling Costs a Dollar

When Owing a Shilling Costs a Dollar

The Saga of Lewis G. Clarke,
Born a "White" Slave

Carver Clark Gayton

To order additional copies of this book, contact:
Xlibris LLC
1-888-795-4274
www.Xlibris.com
Orders@Xlibris.com
622959

Contents

Preface

Some think of history as a subject for the dead and dying. Others think of it as a false recounting by ideologues. Still others, and I count myself among them, find history a living, breathing, and present entity that provides a compass for the future. For that, I blame my mother.

My father and his side of the family were reluctant to talk about past experiences in Yazoo County, Mississippi, before coming to the Northwest. It was a place, event, and circumstance to move beyond and forget. My father's father left the Deep South never to return in either word or deed. It was a place of unspoken shame, of slavery, and later, of sharecropping. My grandfather's decision to move to Seattle was progressive and reflected the tone and timbre of many blacks who left the South at the end of the Reconstruction Era, beginning in the late 1870s. The shackles, at least physically, were broken. Opportunity was waiting for those who took advantage of what he regarded as the American dream that would become a reality for him and his future family in Seattle.[1]

My mother, on the other hand, found solace and affirmation in recalling her family's history, which was hardly that of wealth and material success. Her family story was filled with pride and perseverance despite slavery's indelible imprint. She wanted her children to know that no one could diminish the relevance of her decidedly American family, which could trace its roots to the very beginning of the nation and beyond.[2]

Before I was old enough to attend school, I remember my mother reading stories to the younger siblings, of which I was one. The books she read included those about King Arthur's Court, *Treasure Island* by Robert Louis Stevenson, and Joel Chandler Harris's *Uncle Remus* (based on folklore of African slaves). She also included in her repertoire all the traditional children's fairy tales. While she read, the radio had to be turned off. Very few families had televisions in Seattle homes at the time. I remember the evenings when Mom would ask us questions from the latest issue of *Parents Magazine*. The questions were organized by age of the children up to around eighteen or so. The challenge of those sessions was exciting and fun, but I hated being wrong. Missing an answer made me determined to be correct on the next one.

Invariably the family gatherings led to discussions of African American leaders of the past. Some of them included, among others, the great poet Phyllis Wheatley, who once had an audience with President George Washington; inventor and architect Benjamin Banneker, whose city plans of Washington, DC, were utilized as the model for the current configuration of the nation's capital; abolitionist Frederick Douglass, confidant of presidents Lincoln, Grant, and Garfield; educator and political leader Booker T. Washington; National Association for the Advancement of Colored People (NAACP) founder W. E. B. Du Bois; black nationalist Marcus Garvey; and scientist George Washington Carver, as well as US Patent Office attorney Henry Baker, chronicler of Negro inventors of the nineteenth century.[3]

Books in our home, regarding all of the above, were used as references during the evening conversations with my mother and, from time to time, my father. Few, if any, of these outstanding contributors to American science, culture, and the arts were ever discussed in the schools that I and my brothers and sisters attended.

Included in the conversations regarding black leaders was an African American hero and colleague of Frederick Douglass, Lewis Garrard Clarke, Mom's grandfather. From the bookcase in our living room, I can see her now, pulling out an old careworn book with a plum-red cover entitled *The Key to Uncle Tom's Cabin* by Harriet Beecher Stowe; I learned later that the book was written in response to detractors of *Uncle Tom's Cabin* who were convinced that the story line regarding the harsh treatment of blacks was an exaggeration. *The Key* details examples of real experiences of slaves, including those of Lewis. My mother would turn to the chapter on George Harris, a lead character in Stowe's *Uncle Tom's Cabin*, whom she described as a rebellious runaway slave with white features. *The Key* described Lewis G. Clarke as the prototype for the character George Harris of Stowe's novel.

Not until much later in my life, after greater appreciation of history and considerable research, did I realize he was a true American hero and patriot. Lewis Clarke's story begins with his birth on a plantation in 1815 in Madison County, Kentucky. He was the child of a Scottish Revolutionary War veteran and a quadroon slave. Lewis was taken from his family as a child and forced to live with terribly cruel plantation owners. After being sold to a more compassionate owner, a few years passed when he became fearful of a rumor that he was to be sold to a plantation in Louisiana. At this point, in 1842, Lewis decided to flee from bondage and seek refuge in Canada. He received information that led him to believe his younger brother Milton had escaped to Canada months earlier. Lewis returned to the United States after learning that Milton was living in Oberlin, Ohio. He connected with Milton in Oberlin but soon decided to assist his youngest brother, Cyrus, to flee Kentucky. After rescuing Cyrus, Lewis returned to Oberlin where he and his brother Milton were nearly captured by slave hunters. The incident, which was nationally publicized, convinced them that Ohio was too dangerous. Lewis and Milton decided to leave Ohio to live in Cambridgeport (Cambridge) Massachusetts, where they soon became activists in the abolitionist movement.

Lewis resided for several years in Cambridgeport, home of Aaron Mary Jackson Safford, a sister-in-law of Harriet Beecher Stowe. Lewis met with Stowe at the Safford home on many occasions. According to Clarke, during the meetings, she interviewed him and wrote detailed notes regarding Lewis's experiences as a slave. All the meetings took place years before *Uncle Tom's Cabin* was published in 1852.

While living with the Saffords, Lewis dictated his autobiography, *Narrative of the Sufferings of Lewis Clarke: During a Captivity of More Than Twenty-Five Years among the Algerines of Kentucky, One of the So-Called Christian States of North America, Dictated by Himself,* which was published in 1845. Because of the popularity of the book, it was decided to have a sequel publication that included the slave experiences of his brother Milton. The 1846 dual publication was entitled *Narratives of the Sufferings of Lewis and Milton Clarke, Sons of a Soldier of the Revolution, During a Captivity of More Than Twenty-Five Years among the Slaveholders of Kentucky, One of the So-Called Christian States of North America, Dictated by Themselves.*

The two books were considerably popular during the 1840s with cumulative sales of at least fifteen thousand. The narratives went through two editions in Boston by printer David Ela and two editions in London, England, by Chapman Brothers and Wortley in 1846. The publications are regarded as among the most popular slave narratives ever written. Clarke's many lectures, along with the publications, made him a well-known figure in the Northeast. He shared speaking platforms with the leading abolitionists of the era including his friend Frederick Douglass, as well as Lydia Maria Child, Lewis Tappan, William Lloyd Garrison, Henry Bibb, and Martin Delany, among many others. In view of his popularity during those times, it is reasonable for students of history to ask, "Why then is there so little known or written about Clarke today?" Much of the problem relates to how slave narratives were perceived for many generations.

Many fugitive slaves who wrote or had written slave narratives before the end of slavery were also very popular. Frederick Douglass sold five thousand copies of his narrative within four months of publication in 1845. Solomon Northup's narrative sold twenty-seven thousand in its first two years. The influential theologian Theodore Parker stated in an 1849 speech that our enduring American literature "which is wholly indigenous and original is the literary lives of fugitive slaves. All the original romance of Americans is in them, not in the white man's novel."[4] Charles Sumner, the powerful antislavery US senator from Massachusetts, said in 1852 that "the fugitive slave and their narratives . . . are among the heroes of our age. Romance has no storms of more thrilling interest than theirs. Classical antiquity has preserved no examples of adventurous trial more worthy of renown."[5] With the kind of popularity and key support from leaders of the pre-Civil War years of the narratives, how could they simply disappear for so many years? Some scholars contend that the end of reconstruction in the South in 1876 and the onslaught of apartheid and Black Codes were stark reflections of the economic, political, and social changes taking place throughout the nation. Within the literary world, the result was a "deafening silence of the black voice . . . this led to the destruction of black arts and writings existing before 1865. Only with great devotion and diligence have African Americans begun to restore the pieces of lost records of the mind. Clearly, these losses created an enormous cost to the development of art and literature as well as slave narratives."[6]

For much of the past century, slave narratives have not been given much credence by historians.[7] Many of them, such as Clarke's, were dictated to white abolitionists who were considered zealots and overdramatized the slave's experiences.[8] Although there is some truth to this point, the most logical source to find out about life on the plantation is through the eyes of the slaves reflected in their autobiographies.[9] Because the narratives came from the experiences of black slaves, undoubtedly, many of the earlier historians had an inherited negative bias against the stories. The narratives of slaves such as Frederick Douglass and Harriet Jacobs were given more authenticity because they wrote their own publications, notwithstanding the superlative quality of their books. It is important to note, however, when considering the history of black literature, some of the most powerful and important accounts of black life in America were dictated to others—prime examples being *The Autobiography of Malcolm X,* dictated to Alex Haley, and *His Eye Is on the Sparrow* by Ethel Waters. Yuval Taylor points out that "without these and without the narratives of . . . the Clarke [Lewis and Milton] brothers, Henson, Northup, and John Brown, the world of black literature would be a significantly poorer place."[10]

More recent scholars of the antebellum years of American history and literature such as John Blassingame, C. Peter Ripley, David S. Reynolds, Henry Lewis Gates Jr., and Charles Johnson, have a more positive view concerning the relevance of slave narratives. As a result, the significance of Clarke's story has reemerged after being in fallow for more than one hundred years. Yuval Taylor also explains, "Most slave narratives were written or dictated by escaped slaves before the Civil War" and that "only one to two percent of the slave population escaped. Those who did escape tended to be brave individuals, physically strong, intelligent and creative. Most were literate, had excellent memories and possessed first rate analytical skills."[11] Knowing Clarke's story, one will readily surmise that he embodied many of these characteristics.

By the time Clarke published his narratives, he was a young man of thirty years of age. Clarke's full and exciting life over his remaining fifty years is relatively unknown. Hopefully, this publication will provide a more complete picture of his important contributions to our nation.

In the late 1840s, Lewis moved to the Underground Railroad town of Busti in southwestern New York State. While there, he became a vigilante protector of escaped slaves from the South and continued his lectures across the northern United States as well as Canada. With slave catchers in hot pursuit, Clarke decided to escape to Canada but continued to travel back and forth, surreptitiously, between the US and Canadian border to assist fugitives and participate in meetings relevant to the antislavery movement. During this time, Clarke was selected as president of the local Radical Abolitionist Party located in Sugargrove, Pennsylvania, across the New York border from Busti. By the mid-1850s, Clarke was held in such high esteem he was invited to deliver one of the keynote addresses at the founding convention of the Republican Party in Jackson, Michigan, in July 1854.

Lewis, after moving to Canada, married Emiline Walker from Lexington, Kentucky, and raised a family. In 1874, nine years after the end of the Civil War, Clarke and his family returned to the United States and settled in Oberlin, Ohio. Lewis continued on the lecture circuit throughout the United States, oftentimes mentioning to the press that he had a manuscript of his autobiography. After considerable research, to date, no such document has been found.

During the mid-1890s, an international controversy arose between Lewis and Harriet Beecher Stowe regarding his role as the model for George Harris within *Uncle Tom's Cabin*. Clarke claimed for fifty years that he was a longtime acquaintance of Mrs. Stowe and that she could not have written her book without the information she received from him. With her life ebbing away, however, she and her family representatives denied any knowledge of him, despite extensive reference to Clarke and his narrative in Stowe's 1853 publication *The Key to Uncle Tom's Cabin*. Lewis Clarke's conflict with Mrs. Stowe could have diminished the legitimacy of his contributions to American history; however, his brother Milton's confrontation with the realities of bloodlines and color in America, toward the end of the nineteenth century, not only divided the Clarke family but also contributed toward muting the significance of Lewis Clarke.

We may never know all the factors that led Stowe to renounce her connection with Clarke toward the end of her life. However, an examination of her character and personal motivations reveal some interesting speculations. Nevertheless, Clarke's life as a whole should define his legacy rather than his connection with Harriet Beecher Stowe. His contributions to the abolitionist movement, his unrivaled personal commitment to freeing slaves, and his lifelong dedication to human rights deserve to be celebrated and praised by all Americans.

This publication is a saga about the life of Lewis Clarke. References to subjects such as the antislavery movement, slavery, slave narratives, politics of the nineteenth century, or Harriet Beecher Stowe are discussed within the context of how such references influenced Clarke's life. More in-depth analyses of these important themes can best be done by the many scholars of those fields of study. Some readers may question why much of the author's material on Clarke comes from primary sources such as newspapers, letters, official documents, etc., rather than from secondary or analytical writings. The fact is that scholars did not write about Clarke, particularly during the last fifty years of his life. The negative view of slave narratives by early scholars of the antebellum South, discussed previously, may have turned them away from investigating Clarke more seriously.

Like the life journey of most of us, there is no common theme to Clarke's life but a variety of themes that have common elements. Clarke was devoted to his family and risked his life for his siblings, but some of his children misunderstood his commitment to them. He praised Harriet Beecher Stowe for her great book but was perplexed by her actions toward him. Clarke maintained an unwavering commitment to the betterment of his people despite suffering deep personal tragedies concerning color and bloodlines throughout his life. However, he never gave up on what America, one day, could be.

PART I

Chapter 1

Early Years Of Bondage And Escape

Joseph Lovejoy, to whom Lewis Clarke dictated the story of his life as a slave, first became acquainted with him in December of 1842. Clarke was speaking to an audience of more than one thousand excited people in Hallowell, Maine. He had recently arrived in New England from Ohio by way of his slave home in Kentucky. At the behest of abolitionist leaders, he immediately went on a speaking tour telling large crowds of his vivid recollections of his twenty-five years as a slave. On that cold December day, Lovejoy saw Clarke as a strong and energetic personality with deep religious convictions and an unmistakable commitment to bring down the slave system. The large crowd listened to him with sincere interest. From that day forward, Lovejoy was drawn to him.

After Clarke settled in his new home in Cambridgeport, Massachusetts, Lovejoy noticed how often Lewis became silent and in deep meditation. When asked what he was thinking, he would reply how sad he was about his friends and family still enslaved and suffering in Kentucky and the guilt he had being free. Such bitter recollections of his early life would cause tears to pour down his face. Behind the positive and jovial personality he portrayed to his audiences was a man who was driven by indescribable emotional pain he endured most of his life.

Many who heard Clarke lecture throughout New England encouraged him to record his story in a book, which ultimately led to Clarke dictating his story to Mr. Lovejoy and led to the publication of *Narrative of the Sufferings of Lewis Clarke: During a Captivity of More*

Than Twenty-Five Years among the Algerines of Kentucky, One of the So-Called Christian States of North America, Dictated by Himself.

Much of Clarke's story of his early years in bondage reflected within this chapter derived from Clarke's published *Narrative*. However, his story has been enhanced by the inclusion of revelations and observations from other publications and documents that help clarify and make more vivid his experiences during those years.

Lewis's saga begins with his mother, Letitia or "Letty" Campbell, born out of wedlock to Captain Samuel Campbell, a veteran of the Revolutionary War and a wealthy Kentucky plantation owner.[12] Letitia's mother was Campbell's mulatto slave, Mary. Samuel later became legally married to Mary Anderson Kennedy, a descendant of wealthy slave-owning families. Letty grew up as a slave in the Campbell household of white half-brothers and sisters. According to a granddaughter of Captain Campbell, Mary Ann Banton, Letty was regarded as an "especial favorite" of the Campbell family.[13]

When the early stages of the War of 1812 commenced, Campbell went to the front and left his wife and children at home and felt assured knowing of "Letitia's faithfulness and capability" as a house servant. Before Campbell left, he hired a "humbler countryman," a Scotsman, to be the family weaver. A year went by and Campbell came home and was told by his wife that the weaver, Daniel Clarke, and Letitia were lovers. Campbell ordered Clarke off the plantation and lectured Letitia that terrible things would happen to both of them if they brought scandal upon his name. Campbell left again for a short period of time and returned from the war and found Clarke still on the estate.[14] Another scene took place, and he threatened to cowhide Daniel who told him to do as he pleased because he loved Letitia. "Hoot, toot, man!" exclaimed Campbell. "You're a grand fool. Do you suppose I want a lot of white Negro children on my place? And don't you know your children will be my slaves—that I will put them in my pocket, that I will sell them?" But nothing daunted Clarke, and he married Letitia, vowing her master would never sell her children.[15]

Daniel Clarke was a wounded veteran of the Revolutionary War who, according to his son Lewis, fought in major campaigns in the Northeast and Virginia. Clarke fought as a Minuteman and marched on the alarm of April 19, 1775, to Cambridge with Col. William

Prescott's regiment, which went on to fight in the Battle of Bunker Hill in June of 1775.[16] Having lost a wife in Scotland who left to him two sons, he came to this country to fight with the Colonists.[17] He was a weaver by trade and passed this talent to his son Lewis.[18] Letty bore Daniel nine children, with Lewis being the seventh. One can appreciate the bravery of Daniel not only as a soldier but also for marrying a slave, considering the social mores of that time. Daniel was assured by Campbell, Letty's white father, that she and any of the children born to her would be granted freedom in his will. It was with this promise that Daniel married her; however, that promise was never fulfilled. The only semblance of family life was during the early years of the children. Letty served as the cook in her father's house. Daniel, homesick for Scotland and its legends, often sang folk songs of his native land. Lewis was taught how to spin flax by his father and utilized this skill for work as well as entertainment his entire life. Early on, even though the family was together, their lives were fragile. The children, being the *legitimate* offspring of a free white father and a quadroon mother, one would think these would have been positive factors toward the likelihood of them becoming free. Nevertheless, freedom never came. The disintegration of any semblance of a family began when Lewis was the age of six. He unexpectedly fell into the hands of one of Grandfather Campbell's daughters, Betsey Campbell Banton.

As was the custom of the day, a woman who married would be provided a young slave as part of her dowry. When Betsey married, of two slaves given to her, one died and the other was sold after suffering mental and physical abuse by her. At the wedding of Betsey's sister Polly, the same process took place with Polly receiving two healthy slaves. The cantankerous Betsey exclaimed, "Poll has a girl and a boy, and I only had that fool girl. I reckon if I go home without a boy too, this house won't be left standing." The threat led to all the young slave boys of the household being marched before Betsey for her to choose. Betsey selected Lewis. Lewis's grandfather Campbell objected because the selection would divide the family. In an attempt to compromise, Grandfather Campbell offered another child whose parents were sold to a plantation further South. The shrill and ranting voice of Mrs. Banton dominated the discussion, and Lewis became the property of the evil mistress. The old and sickly grandfather left the home in disgust to drive away bad thoughts. Young Lewis, seeing the anguish in his mother's

eyes but not fully understanding the circumstances, was taken away
in the Bantons' carriage the following morning. Samuel Campbell
died in 1821, soon after the Bantons took possession of Lewis.[19] The
will within which he promised the freedom of Letitia and her children
was never found. After Samuel's death, the Campbell heirs gathered to
divide the estate. More than likely the will was found and destroyed
by the heirs. The market value of the slaves was probably too tempting
to disregard. The Clarke family began to be divided among the white
children of Campbell. Letty and her family were included in the assets
of the estate, in spite of the angry interference of one of the daughters,
Judith Campbell Logan. "Letty is our own half-sister and you know it,"
she protested to her brothers and sisters. "You know Father never meant
that she and her children would be sold." Letty's husband, Daniel, now
old and ill, was outraged. Having fought for his country's freedom from
British rule, he said bitterly, "Must I now see my wife and children sold
in this free country?"[20] The pleas from both Daniel Clarke and Judith
Logan were ignored. The auction proceeded, and mother and children
were sold at prices ranging from $300 to $800 and relocated to different
plantations in Kentucky.[21] Lewis's mother, Letitia, as well as his sister,
Delia, and brothers, Milton and Cyrus, were sold to the Joseph and
Judith Logan family.

Lewis, separated earlier from his mother and siblings, remained
the slave of Betsey Campbell Banton and her husband John.[22] During
the ten years Lewis spent with the Bantons, he was allowed to see his
family only three times. He described that period of his life as his most
miserable and lonely years. Letty, on occasion, was able to send her son
some token of affection such as an apple or sugar plum. He lamented,
"I scarcely ever ate them, they were laid up and handled and wept over
till they wasted away in my hand." Imagining a young child endure such
suffering is heart wrenching. The beatings and whippings from Mrs.
Banton were constant. Her tools of torture were usually the rawhide or
a bunch of hickory sprouts seasoned by fire and tied together.

By the age of nine Lewis began to spin flax and hemp. He worked
from dawn to dusk. Being exhausted by the end of each day it was
impossible for him to stay awake. Mrs. Banton would throw dippers
full of vinegar and salt into his sleepy eyes. Lewis pointed out, "Mrs.
Banton, as is common among slave holding women, seemed to hate
and abuse me all the more because I had the blood of her father in my

veins." Additionally, her husband was known to drive hot nails into the back of a slave who worked in the blacksmith shop who, on occasion, displeased him.

Lewis witnessed even more horrendous treatment of slaves outside of the Banton plantation. He watched as a runaway slave named Tom was caught by an overseer and whipped three hundred lashes.[23] Lewis described how he had the job of washing his back with salt and water. He said Tom's "flesh crawled, crept, and quivered under his hands." Slave owners initiated this approach to whippings, according to Lewis, in order to make the slaves "smart," that is, make it painful enough so the slave would think twice before committing any other rebellious actions and also to prevent "mortification," i.e., infection, in the lacerated flesh.[24]

Punishments levied against slave women were just as harsh as those suffered by the men. A slave employed as a driver on the plantation, was forced to whip his own wife for killing her pig and never recovered. She literally was whipped to death by her own husband. The worst kind of torture Lewis witnessed in Kentucky was seeing a slave woman stripped naked and hung up by her hands and whipped till blood ran down her back.[25] This act was even more degrading when it was done by a young master or mistress to an aged mother, or even a grandmother. Clarke said that "nothing the slaves abhor as they do this." One can imagine the feelings of degradation, not only by the women being beaten but their grieving children and grandchildren who witnessed such atrocities.

A poignant and heartbreaking story, which Clarke included in many of his lectures and speeches for the antislavery cause, was described by him: "Preacher Raymond didn't used to flog his slaves, he used to duck 'em. He had a little slave girl, about eight years old, that he used to 'duck' very often. One day the family went to a meeting and left her to take care of the young child. The child fretted, and she thought she would serve it as master served her, so she ducked it, and it slipped out of her hands and got drowned. They put her in prison and sentenced her to be hung, but she, poor child, didn't know nothing at all what it meant. When they took her to the gallows, she was guarded all around by men, but she was so innocent, she didn't know what they were going to do with her. She stooped to pick up a pin and stuck it in her frock as she went. The poor young thing was so glad to get out of prison that she was as merry as if she were going to her mother's house."[26]

In Clarke's written narration, he presented his stories about his life as a slave with a unique blend of sarcasm, bitterness, pathos, and comedy. All those characteristics are reflected in his anecdote of the slave named George. George was the property of a man of high standing in the local church. The old gentleman was taken sick, and the doctor told him he would die. He called George and said if he would wait upon him attentively and do everything for him possible, he would remember him in his will; he would do something handsome for him. George was very much excited to know what it might be; he hoped it might be in the heart of the master to give him his freedom. At last the will was made. George was still more excited. The master noticed it and asked what the matter was. "Massa, you promise do something in your will. Poor nigger! What Massa done for George?"

"O, George, don't be concerned. I have done a very handsome thing for you—such as any slave would be proud to have done for him." This did not satisfy George. He was still very eager to know what it was.

At length the master saw it necessary to tell George, to keep him quiet and make him attend to his duty. "Well, George, I have made provision that when you die, you shall have a good coffin and be put in the same vault with me. Will that not satisfy you, George?"

"Well, Massa, one way I am satisfied and one way I am not."

"What? What?" said the old master. "What is the matter with that?"

"Why . . ." said George, "I like to have a good coffin when I die."

"Well, don't you like to be in the same vault with me and other rich masters?"

"Why, yes, Massa, one way I like it and one way I don't."

"Well, what don't you like?"

"Why I 'fraid, Massa, when de debbil come take you body, he make mistake and take mine."[27]

Clarke explained that slaves preferred to be buried at the greatest possible distance from the master. They were superstitious and feared that the slave driver, having whipped them so much when alive, would somehow beat them when dead.

After ten years with the Bantons, Lewis was sold because of financial difficulties resulting from John Banton's involvement in a counterfeiting plot. General Thomas Kennedy of Garrard County, Kentucky, near the village of Paint Lick, became Lewis's new master. Kennedy fought in the

War of Independence and came to Kentucky in about 1780, fighting the Indians along the way. General Kennedy owned seven thousand acres of land and one hundred and fifty slaves.[28] He was enormously wealthy for those days. Lewis, in his 1845 narrative, referred to Kennedy as Mr. K because of fear, after his escape from slavery, that "he or any other man should ever claim *property* where they never had any." He said that his circumstances improved greatly from what he experienced under the Bantons. Although in his new situation he had more freedom and less cruelty, "it was far from enviable."[29]

The whipping death of Uncle Tom in Harriet Beecher Stowe's book was suggested by the fate of Sam Peter, a blacksmith on General Kennedy's plantation who, because of a small offense, was swung up by his hands to the limbs of a locust tree by Kennedy, an overseer as well as a waiter, and whipped in turn by each with several hundred lashes, and two months later, Sam was dead.[30] The whipping death of Uncle Tom in Harriet Beecher Stowe's *Uncle Tom's Cabin* reflects almost identical circumstances leading to the death of Sam Peter. Clarke heard him say to his mother in almost the exact words uttered by old Tom: "Mother, tell Master he has killed me at last, for nothing, but tell him if God will forgive him, I can."

Clarke asserted that the character of Uncle Tom in Stowe's book was based upon the experiences of three slaves: Sam Peter as noted above, J. Banton (no relation to the white Bantons of Kentucky), and Reverend Josiah Henson of Dawn, Ontario, Canada. All were acquaintances of Clarke while in Kentucky. The character of the evil Simon Legree was based, in part, on General Thomas Kennedy. General Kennedy's daughter, Nancy Kennedy Letcher, knew Lewis well before his escape from Kentucky and confirmed the existence of Sam Peter in an 1881 interview. However, Nancy could not fathom her father treating Sam in such a manner.[31]

In 1836, General Kennedy died, and after the division of the estate, Lewis became the slave of Thomas Kennedy Jr., the general's son. The young Kennedy found it more profitable to hire out Lewis's time. This meant he would board and clothe himself and turn whatever he earned to his master. Lewis was allowed to travel around on horseback with an open pass, selling grass seed, splitting rails, trading, and weaving, paying his master $12 a month. For Lewis, this taste of freedom made him contemplate the possibility of true and full liberty.

Of all that Lewis experienced or witnessed during captivity, the tragic experiences of his sister Delia had the most long-lasting impact on him. Holding back tears during one interview, he said, "Hers was a most bitter and tragic history." Lewis described her as being, to her detriment, "uncommonly beautiful." As she grew into her early years as a woman, she was considered a great prize for the passions of the plantation owners. Delia became the "property" of a tanner by trade named Joseph Logan, as were Lewis's mother, Letitia, and his brothers, Milton and Cyrus. Joseph married one of the daughters of Samuel Campbell, the good-hearted Judith Campbell. After Judith died, Joseph intended to make Delia his mistress. She rejected his intentions repeatedly. Her mother, Letitia, told her she should commit suicide rather than submit to him. Logan whipped Delia often because of her rejections. On one occasion during a beating, Letitia begged Joseph not to kill her. He turned around and knocked Letitia down and continued to beat Delia. Milton, witnessing the beatings, ran to a shed and grabbed an ax to kill Logan. Letitia stopped Milton just in time; otherwise Logan would have killed him.

Thwarted in his attempts to seduce Delia, Logan decided to sell her and sent her to New Orleans where she was kept for four weeks and then put up for sale. Blacks in Kentucky considered slave owners in Louisiana and Mississippi to be among the most evil in the United States. Before the sale, Delia had her hair styled and was furnished with a new dress. Everything was done to make the beautiful young lady even more stunning. The bidding started off at a low of $500 but became exceptionally brisk and ultimately went up to $1,600. Fortunately, Delia went into the hands of a kind Frenchman named Coval, who emancipated her, and they subsequently married. The couple traveled extensively, visiting Mexico, the West Indies, and France, where they lived for more than a year. After four or five years of marriage, her husband died, leaving a fortune of twenty to thirty thousand dollars.[32]

Soon after the sale of Delia, the father of Joseph Logan, Deacon Archibald Logan, purchased Joseph's estate in Lexington, including mother Letitia, and Lewis's brothers, Cyrus and Milton. Because of Joseph's ill heath, he could not maintain his property. Three or four years after the transaction, Joseph came to his father's home sick with consumption and soon died. Milton then became the Deacon's "body servant."

Letitia Clarke died in 1833 from the cholera epidemic that spread throughout Kentucky that year. Lewis, being on a separate plantation was not allowed to attend her funeral. Daniel perished a few years earlier. Milton experienced considerable despair and loneliness after the death of his mother. However, Milton's outlook on life was bolstered when Deacon Logan allowed him considerable freedom by loaning him out to make money from his various skills. Milton was especially adept as a musician and performed as a drummer and bugler with a variety of bands. Logan allowed Milton to be hired out by the day or week. However, Milton had to give the deacon three dollars and a half a day from his earnings. Milton did not like the arrangement and convinced the deacon to allow him a greater percentage of his earnings. Milton began saving some of his money and was enjoying the good fortune. He soon realized he could take care of himself. The true meaning of the Declaration of Independence and Liberty became clear to him. Milton mused, "I could never reason myself into the belief that the old deacon had any right to the annual rent which I paid for my own body." Milton was paying Deacon Logan two hundred dollars a year for his time, boarding, and clothes. Milton decided that the unjust arrangement had to end. He was determined to find some to way to attain his freedom.

In 1838, Milton was hired out by Deacon Logan to play with a musical group on the Ohio and Mississippi rivers. He visited New Orleans several times and attempted to meet with Delia each time he was there. Through an old acquaintance he located Delia's residence. He went to her house and told her he was her younger brother. She did not believe him because he had grown a great deal between the years they last saw each other. To test Milton's identity, she showed him a small piece of cloth and asked if he had ever seen it before. Milton replied that it once belonged to their mother Letitia. "Ah! Then," she said, "you really are my brother."[33]

The following summer, Delia and Milton visited Kentucky and stayed several months. While in Kentucky, she made a partial payment for the freedom of their brother Dennis. As soon as Delia returned to New Orleans, she sent Dennis the balance. She also intended to purchase from Deacon Logan the freedom of brothers Milton and Cyrus. During the autumn of 1840, Milton started on a trip to New Orleans from Kentucky to pick up the money promised by Delia. After arriving in Louisville, he was given a letter indicating that Delia had died. The letter also stipulated that Delia's property in New Orleans was to go to Milton and utilized to purchase his freedom as well as Cyrus's. After arriving in New Orleans, Milton learned from a Louisiana state government official that since Delia's assets were in real estate, the property could not be sold to him because slaves were not citizens.[34] At that point, Milton realized that the option of purchasing his freedom was not likely.

Milton returned to Kentucky in the summer of 1841 and met in Louisville with three slaves he had known over the years, named Henry, Reuben, and George, who like him were good musicians. The three slaves begrudgingly gave a significant amount of the money they earned to their master, Doctor Graham of Harrodsburg, Kentucky. Due to the recent heartbreaking news of Delia's estate, Milton was convinced that he had to follow through with his intent to break away from Deacon Logan. Milton challenged the slaves, "Now, boys, is the time to strike for liberty. I go for Ohio tomorrow. What say you?" The slaves pondered Milton's question briefly and then agreed that they should go to Cincinnati where they had already scheduled to perform for a high-society ball. After performing at the ball, friends there advised Milton and his fellow musicians to go further north. Doctor Graham's slaves decided to continue on to Canada, but Milton opted out, preferring to stop in Oberlin to take part in that city's thriving abolitionist movement.[35]

While in Oberlin, Milton assisted escaped slaves in their journey toward Canada. Milton sarcastically observed, "The masters accused me of *stealing* several of them [slaves]. This is a great lie. I never stole one in my life. I have assisted several to get into possession of the true owner, but I never assisted any man to steal another away from himself. God has given every man true title to himself, written upon his face." Milton remained in Oberlin during the summer of 1841.[36]

Circumstances for Lewis on young Thomas Kennedy's plantation were such that he soon became committed to escape north to Canada. This Kennedy was not particularly bright, but not as cruel as his father. He certainly had more freedom while enslaved by young Kennedy, but he was still considered property, which Clarke would never recognize. His young master died in 1840. The administrators of the estate, a Judge John Letcher, the son-in-law of General Kennedy, and a Mr.

Bridges hired Clarke out for a while but soon decided to put him up for sale. No bid could be obtained for Lewis.

According to Clarke there were two reasons that hindered the transaction. One was there were two or three old mortgages on the property that were not settled, and the second reason given by the bidders was he had too many privileges, such as being permitted to trade for himself and allowed to travel all over Kentucky. In other words, Clarke said he was considered a "spoilt nigger." Clarke agreed. For their purposes he was indeed proud being considered a "spoilt nigger." Clarke began to think long and hard about seeking liberty. The challenges that he faced were overwhelming. If he failed in his efforts, he would be disrespected by other slaves, beaten unmercifully by his master, and then watched and worked harder the rest of his life. On the other hand, if he got away, what would he do? What would he find? Clarke could not read or write and was fundamentally ignorant of the world. How could he adjust to a completely foreign environment? All the white people he knew were enemies to him and all slaves. His masters told him that abolitionists decoyed escaped slaves to the free states and then sold them to Louisiana or Mississippi, and if he went to Canada, the British would put out his eyes and place him in a underground mine where he would work for the rest of his life. How would he know whom or what to believe? Clarke had no comprehension at all what was before him once he escaped. These kinds of questions faced most slaves contemplating breaking away from slavery. Those who did so had to be unusually self-confident, brave, and physically fit, with a burning desire not to continue to be victimized by an unjust system of servitude. Clarke thought long and hard before making up his mind to flee.

After several months, whispers floating around the plantation indicated he was finally to be sold to a slave owner in Louisiana. Lewis was notified to be present at the Garrard County Courthouse in Lancaster, the county seat, in two weeks to complete the settlement of the estate. John Letcher's house girl overheard the administrator William Bridges and two slave traders, Messrs. Chinneway and Lawless bargaining for Lewis and three other slaves named Jim, Steve, and Mose. All were to be taken down the river to Louisianna after the transaction at the courthouse in Lancaster. Hearing of his impending sale made him decide unequivocally to make his move. Concurrently, Lewis overheard that his brother Milton had escaped to Canada with the group of musicians with whom he was performing. This rumor gave him additional resolve to fulfill his dream.

Clarke's initial plan was concocted between him and a slave named Ross Isaac. Isaac proposed to take his mistress's horse, and Clarke was to take his pony, and they were to ride off together. They started north from Garrard County, Kentucky, on horseback.[37] Because of Lewis's light skin, they tried to pose as master and body servant and had gone only a few miles when Clarke decided to turn back because he realized that he did not think through all the obstacles they would face. Clarke had no idea how to manage a servant, and keen observers would see through their awkwardness. Additionally, neither knew the roads well enough, nor could they read the road signs. Isaac pled with Clarke to continue with their plan, to no avail. Clarke felt sorry for Isaac but decided that their plan, although creative, would lead to failure.[38] The idea of leaving Kentucky as a gentleman with a servant was not far-fetched. Lewis passed as a white man everywhere in the vicinity except with those who knew him as a slave. While in flight he never had to use his pass as a seed peddler, nevertheless, the threat of being discovered consumed him.

He and Ross Issac returned to the plantation. On a Saturday in August of 1841, he saddled his horse, placed his clothes in his saddlebags, and them into grass seed bags. He wore a wide rimmed fur hat and other clothes attempting to portray himself as a gentleman farmer. However, his disguise did not settle his nerves, imagining that the administrator of the plantation was watching him. Lewis then set out alone on his horse about fifty miles south of Lexington. Within the *Narrative,* Clarke did not reveal the exact place where he departed for fear of slave catchers discovering the spot; however, it is clear he left near the town of Paint Lick which is in proximity to the Kennedy plantation. What a day it was for him. His emotions ran the gamut from euphoria to fear, but he would not turn back from this second attempt to flee.

After riding approximately fifteen miles, he came across a Baptist minister he knew on the road, who said, "How do you do, boy? Are you free? I always thought you were free till I saw them trying to sell you the other day." He admonished Lewis by saying, "Servants obey their masters."

Clarke, taken aback, finally replied, "What makes you think I was free?"

He replied that he noticed Clarke had great privileges, that he did as much as he liked, and that he was almost white.

Clarke countered, "Oh yes, but there are a great many slaves as white as I am."

The minister said yes and went on to name several who had lately run away. Clarke said to himself, this conversation was touching too close to what he was in the process of doing. He feared that the minister knew in fact that he was running away.[39]

Clarke untruthfully indicated to the old man that he knew nothing of the slaves he mentioned who ran away. Clarke became more relieved when the minister said, "I suppose you would not run away on any account because you are so well treated." Clarke said, "I do very well, very well, sir. If you should ever hear that I had run away, be certain it must be because there is some great change in my treatment," which was indeed a very true statement.

The minister began to talk about buying some grass seed he assumed Clarke had in the bags where he was carrying his clothes. But he changed his mind and rode off. After this close encounter, Clarke thought to himself, *Although I have heard people say poor company is better than none, I feel much better without him than with him.*[40]

As Lewis approached Lexington, he went into a deep valley by the side of the road to change his clothes. Reaching Lexington at about seven o'clock in the evening, he stayed at the home of his youngest brother, Cyrus, also a slave, and his freeborn wife. Lewis had been to Lexington often in the past, residing with Cyrus. Seeing him there would not cause any excitement from slaveholders. Additionally, he still had a pass from his administrator of the Kennedy plantation who hired out his time. He stayed with Cyrus for a day, and they talked about a great many plans if his escape were successful. Both he and his brother were not knowledgeable of the roads and of the best ways to avoid suspicion. After he and Cyrus talked into the night, Lewis wondered how any slave so bereft of information and self-assurance makes the attempt to seek his freedom.

The following Monday morning, Lewis set his sights on reaching the village of Mayslick located twenty miles from the Ohio River and fifty miles from Lexington. Just before reaching the town that evening, he stopped to think over his situation. His horse was worn out and unable to reach the river that night. Lewis also concluded that it would be too dangerous to attempt to cross that night because it would arouse suspicion. He decided to spend the night in Mayslick but was unsure of what course to take. At first he thought of taking his horse into a field close to the town to give him some corn while he slept in the grass. But then the slave-hunting dogs would be out in the evening, and if caught under such circumstances with a pony, he could be considered a thief rather than a runaway. That would not do. Considering the options, Clarke decided to go into the heart of the village and stay in the local tavern.

After taking his horse to the tavern's livery stable, Lewis looked into the bar and was horrified to see several men from his home area who would know him. He had to think fast. He looked across the street from the tavern and saw a silversmith shop. He figured that a pair of glasses would help disguise him. He went to the shop and bartered with the owner for a pair of thick green-glass spectacles. When he put them on, he could barely see. He stumbled back to the tavern and ordered dinner. He had no appetite whatsoever but had the meal to avoid notice. He had a hard time measuring distances with his "new eyes," and on the first attempt to eat from his plate with his knife and fork, the food landed in his lap. He did not need any attention drawn to him, and after drinking a cup of tea, he went immediately to bed. He could not sleep that night. He was trembling, confused, and anxious.

The next morning, Lewis called for his horse, paid his bill, and was on his way, rejoicing that the previous night was over. By noon that day, he crossed the Ohio River by ferry and was in Aberdeen, Ohio. Clarke best described his feelings that moment: "I trembled all over with deep emotion, and I could feel my hair rise up on my head. I was on what was called *free* soil, among people who had no slaves . . . everything was new and wonderful." Not knowing where to find a friend, being in an unfamiliar land, and not willing to make inquiries for fear of revealing his ignorance, it took Lewis a whole week to reach Cincinnati. At one place where he stayed, people asked him more questions than he wanted to answer. At another place where he was rooming, the landlord made it a point to give every guest newspapers. Evidently Lewis was looking at the paper in a peculiar manner and the man felt obligated to point out him the important news of the day. Clarke declined his assistance and gave the paper back, saying his eyes were bothering him.[41]

While at a tavern, a few of the patrons heard that Clarke was from Kentucky and began inquiring, in a very direct manner, about his business background. Clarke had learned that Kentuckians often came to the establishment to kidnap escaped slaves. He satisfied their sharp questioning by assuring them he was not a slaveholder, nor was his father, but before they got too aroused, he added that his grandfather was a slaveholder. Lewis's grandfather, Samuel Campbell, was indeed a slaveholder.

When in Cincinnati, he came across a few acquaintances and had some light conversation with them. On several occasions, he saw a well-known slave dealer from Kentucky who knew him. Clarke consciously kept a distance from him. The only advice he received in the city was from a man who was once a slave. He urged Clarke to sell his horse and to go up the Ohio River to Portsmouth, Ohio, and then take the canal (the Ohio and Erie Canal) for Cleveland, and cross over to Canada. Clarke acted upon his suggestion, sold his horse for a small amount (since the animal was in a frail condition), took passage to Portsmouth, and was soon on the canal boat headed to Cleveland. While on the canal boat, Lewis became acquainted with a man named Mr. Conoly from New York. The man was very ill with a fever, and Clarke made a point to look after him the best he could during the long trip. One day during a conversation, the man began talking about slaves in the harshest manner and was especially critical of runaway slaves. Clarke decided that it would be best to curtail his relationship with Mr. Conoly. His experience with the New Yorker led him to make this astute observation: "I found the *spirit* of slaveholding was not all South of the Ohio River."[42]

Soon after arriving in Cleveland, Lewis encountered a serious problem. As he was entering the tavern where he had reservations, a rough-looking man came running up to him, declaring that he had passed a bad five-dollar bill to his wife while they were on the boat and was demanding silver for the same amount. The travelers who had just arrived at the hotel were asked by the clerk to give their names to enter them into the register. The clerk asked for Lewis's name just as the threatening man was in the middle of his assault on Clarke. When Clarke had left Kentucky, he thought it best to take on a new name, and he entered the boat as Archibald Campbell. Since this man was making a charge against him, he realized it would be disastrous to give a different name than the one he had used on the boat. However, at that moment, Clarke could not recall what he called himself. He was completely puzzled for a few minutes. The clerk kept asking for his name while Clarke was pretending to be deaf. Suddenly the name popped back into his head and Lewis was enrolled as a guest of the hotel. Clarke quipped to himself, "I had heard before of persons being frightened out of their *Christian* names, but I was fairly scared out of both mine for a while."[43] The hotel manager protected Lewis from the potential violence of the crazed man and drove him away from the establishment.

Clarke remained in Cleveland for several days, ruminating about how to get across Lake Erie into Canada. He went to the shore of the lake repeatedly trying to see some kind of landmark on the other side to convince him it was Canada. Clarke was hesitant to inquire, fearing his ignorance would betray him. One day, he overheard a man ask another employed on board a vessel, "Where does this vessel trade?" The question gave him confidence, feeling if it was a proper question for the man it would be for him also. The answer was, "Over there in Kettle Creek, near Port Stanley." Clarke asked "Where is that?" The man replied, "Oh, over there in Canada." The captain asked Lewis if he wanted passage to Canada. He told him he was considering going if he could get cheap passage. Clarke worked out a mutual understanding, and they set sail. After sailing only nine miles, the wind changed, and the captain had to return to the Cleveland port. Clarke considered this a very bad omen. However, he waited to sail again the next evening at nine o'clock and by daylight the boat docked in Canada.

When he stepped ashore he could say at last, "*I am free.*" Not until then "did I dare to cherish, for a moment, the feeling that one of the limbs of my body was my own. My hands, my feet were now my own. But what to do with them was the next question. A strange sky was over me, a new earth under me, strange voices all around. I was entirely alone, no human being that I had ever seen before, where I could speak to him or he to me."[44]

For a time, fear and loneliness consumed him. Kentucky slaveholders had told their slaves that Canadians would blind runaways and force them to work in the coal mines. They said the redcoats would skin the heads of escaped slaves and wear the wool around their necks for collars.[45]

Lewis, while in fear of becoming a victim of the redcoats, searched the area attempting to find Milton. In Chatham, he saw a sight that finally diminished his fears: two black soldiers driving a white prisoner, with his hands bound, ahead of them. Finally he met an old friend named Henry, the former fellow band member with Milton. His conversation with Henry provided the correct information concerning the whereabouts of Milton. Clarke had known that Milton left Kentucky a year before he did. However, Henry told Lewis that Milton was in Oberlin, Ohio.

While in Chatham, Lewis hired himself out to build up his diminishing funds. He had $64 when he left Kentucky and was living off it for six weeks. His employer, Mr. Everett, treated him well and encouraged him to stay in Canada, offering him employment on his farm. He cautioned Lewis, "There is no 'free state' in America, all are *slave* states, bound to slavery, and the slave could have no asylum in any of them." Clarke agreed with Mr. Everett, "I have *felt* wherever I may be in the United States, the kidnappers may be upon me at any moment. If I could creep up to the top of the monument on Bunker Hill, beneath which my father fought, I should not be safe, even there." Mr. Everett's words were seared in his mind throughout the years before the Civil War.

Lewis soon made his way to Sandwich, Ontario, and crossed over to Detroit on his way to Ohio to see Milton. While in Canada, Lewis sold his pistol for a watch. In the process of loading his luggage on the boat to Cleveland, he discovered that he had lost his watch. He immediately dashed back to Sandwich looking for the timepiece. In the meantime, the steamboat bound for Cleveland had departed with his luggage still on board. Most of his money was in his luggage. Failing to find his watch and discovering the boat had left and being low in funds, he boarded a steamer destined for Cleveland and told the captain of his financial plight and convinced him to take him on credit. After docking, he was relieved to find his luggage secure at the wharf. [46]

Finally, the next morning, Lewis was on the stagecoach to Oberlin. Several abolitionists were also passengers. They mentioned that a slave named Milton Clarke was living in Oberlin and that he had a brother in Canada and that he was expecting him to arrive soon. They talked about Milton and of other slaves in a very positive manner, so after a long conversation, Lewis considered them to be friendly and decided to introduce himself. Clarke was surprised and elated by the kindness of the gentlemen and "thought there must be some new principle at work here, such as I had not seen much of in Kentucky." He enjoyed his journey to Oberlin and looked forward to what awaited him at his new home.[47]

    Lewis Clarke's escape from slavery in Kentucky was verified years later by Nancy Kennedy Letcher, Tom Kennedy's sister and daughter of General Thomas Kennedy. However, she had a few fascinating recollections of his hair-raising venture that were contrary to what Clarke recalled. She described Lewis's last days on the plantation as follows: "It happened in this way. My brother Tom, Lewis' master, died and Lewis was seized with fear that he would be sold and taken south. There was little authority for his fears. My husband and my brother-in-law, Mr. Bridges, were the administrators of my brother's estate. They found out that a sale would have to take place, and in talking the matter over one day in the house they were overheard by some nurse girls [slaves] who immediately reported it to the [slave] cabins. Lewis heard it and was greatly frightened. . . . The dread of life in the South then was the greatest felt by any Kentucky Negro. Lewis, to avoid the supposed fate, ran away. He still kept his pass, and was enabled to reach the [Ohio] river by means of it. He afterwards in a letter confessed it to me."[48] No mention was made in his *Narrative* of having been married or leaving a wife and child behind.[49] However, Mrs. Letcher indicated that Lewis had a "wife" named Margy and that they had a beautiful child named Elmada. But Lewis took neither with him, nor did he make any effort to have them join him. Mrs. Letcher went on to say that "from a letter he sent me some time afterwards, it appeared that he had forgotten them entirely." In an August 1896 article, a houseboy of Mrs. Letcher's brother, Norman Kennedy, indicated that he knew Lewis well and verified Mrs. Letcher's account regarding Lewis' relationship with Margy, although he called her Maggie.[50] He said that Maggie was left behind but soon ran off to Louisville with her child. "She secreted herself in Falls City [Louisville] until Clarke returned from Ohio. She joined him there, and the two went up the Ohio River by steam boat to Cincinnati. Maggie, in the eyes of Mrs. Letcher and Norman, was the Eliza in Harriet Beecher Stowe's novel and the wife of George Harris (Lewis Clarke). Readers of *Uncle Tom's Cabin* will remember Eliza's dramatic escape across ice floes of the Ohio River as one of the most thrilling episodes of the novel. In August 1880, a Chicago reporter asked Clarke if he had any recollection of who Eliza in the novel could have been. He replied, "There was such a woman. She crossed the Ohio in 1841—the same winter I was in Oberlin. The river was full of floating cakes of ice at the time. She left one of the child's garments on the bank, so those seeing it would think that she and the child were drowned. I knew Levi Coffin [Quaker abolitionist] and his wife Catherine, who gave her a change of clothing and cared for her after she landed." No references to the woman were ever made by Clarke during his lifetime about any intimate relationship with Maggie despite eyewitness accounts to the contrary.[51]

Mrs. Letcher was asked if she remembered the time when Lewis left the plantation. She replied, "Very well. I believe, indeed, I surprised him with his preparations. Although he had a wife, he had his washing done by one of the women who was a servant about the house. He was very particular about his toilet. I have supposed that his wife could not please him in that regard. One morning I got up a little earlier than usual, and stepping out of my room, saw Lewis passing by, holding a bundle in his hands. I asked him what he held. He replied 'Nothing, ma'am, but my clean shirts,' and passed on in the direction of his cabin. I afterwards learned that he was gone, and I have no doubt that the bundle he was carrying was part of the preparation for his journey."[52]

After arriving in Oberlin during the autumn of 1841, Lewis at last found Milton living at a boarding house of a Mrs. Cole.[53] Lewis had not seen Milton for over a year and, predictably, their reunion was joyous. Mrs. Cole and many of her friends were active in the abolitionist movement. Arrangements were made for Lewis to reside with another local abolitionist, John Eels.

After much urging by Mr. Eels, Lewis finally consented to speak to a large gathering of the Anti-Slavery Society in Oberlin. To make Lewis feel at ease, Mr. Eels asked him questions rather than have him deliver a formal address. After speaking for a while, Clarke was more at ease and commenced to speak for two hours. However, Lewis admitted that because of his lack of education "I made a bad mess of my grammar and was laughed at several times." Nevertheless he won over the crowd with his sincerity and wit. At the close of the address, the society gave him loud applause and voted to give him a monetary donation. Lewis would later utilize the donation to help bring his brother Cyrus out of Lexington, Kentucky. Lewis's Oberlin appearance represented one of the first speeches made in the United States by a runaway slave pleading for his enslaved brothers and sisters. He predated Frederick Douglass in this regard.[54]

Lewis and Milton had a respite in Oberlin during the early months of 1842 making speeches about their exploits to mostly small gatherings of sympathetic abolitionists in the surrounding community. Milton suggested that they move to Massachusetts. Boston was known as a center of the antislavery movement and was certainly a topic of discussion among abolitionists in Oberlin. Northeastern abolitionists such as Lewis and Arthur Tappan and Theodore Weld were known in the area for their financial support of Oberlin College and other abolitionist causes in Ohio and certainly influenced the brothers. Lewis was not enthused about Milton's proposal, indicating that it would be safer to stay in Oberlin with its large numbers of abolitionists. Milton assured him that in Massachusetts, the abolitionists were more numerous than in Ohio. Before making any final decision on Milton's proposal, Lewis's primary interest was to rescue his youngest brother, Cyrus, from slavery in Lexington, Kentucky. Lewis had been deliberating such a plan for months.

As Lewis made arrangements for his trek south, Milton mentioned to him that after his escape he wrote to his master, Deacon Logan, saying that he need not worry about him; he had enough experience to take care of himself. Milton pointed out to the deacon that his care was not worth the two hundred dollars a year Milton was paying him. Milton haughtily chastised the deacon by saying if he remained quiet and content, he should not have any problems without him. Lewis knowingly cautioned that Milton's letter and the escape of two slaves from the same family and the same state would surely raise the ire of the deacon and other slaveholders in Kentucky.

John Eels's wife prepared Lewis for his journey to Kentucky by teaching him to read guidebooks and maps. Lewis did not tell more than three people in Oberlin of his intention to bring Cyrus north.[55] There were many slaves in the town and he was fearful that word of his rescue attempt would get back to Kentucky through them. He left Oberlin on foot in July of 1842 with twenty dollars in his pocket. On his way South destined for Kentucky, Clarke talked with several well-known friends of slaves. Most of them pointed out the dangers he would face and urged him not to go. Only one young man encouraged him to leave, assuring him that God would be by his side. He realized the risks he was taking, but he did not anticipate all the mental anguish and physical pain he would suffer by the end of his 300 mile journey to Lexington.

Reaching the state border village of Ripley on the Ohio River, he met a man who encouraged him to continue moving forward as well as advising him about the roads in Kentucky. He told Lewis there would be less chance of him running into problems if he stayed on the less-traveled roads. The man also gave him a crude map for assistance. Lewis crossed the river at Ripley, and when he reached the other side; he immediately began to tremble and shudder, recalling all that he had suffered over so many years in Kentucky. He became completely overcome with emotion by the thought of reliving those experiences and began to cry uncontrollably. It took an hour before he could compose himself and move forward. In the afternoon of the first day, he took time to bathe and cool his feet. A man rode up on horseback and entered into a long conversation with Lewis and began asking him questions, many of which he evaded. The man pointed out to Clarke that a white lady lived down the road and was recently visited by eight escaped slaves who asked her for food. The experience horrified the woman. The man told Lewis he hoped the slaves would not be captured and expressed his distaste of slavery, saying it was "the curse of Kentucky." He went on to say he was brought up to work and liked it, but slavery made it disgraceful for any white man to work. At first Clarke thought he could trust the man but then decided not to. He concluded, from the conversation that a hundred or so dollars for returning a slave, for a poor man, is a heavy temptation. There was no need to entice the man any further.[56]

As Clarke approached Lexington, he was sore all over his body and decided to hire a horse and carriage for the last seven miles of his trek. As he entered the city on a Sunday afternoon, he observed that there were many people out and about on horseback and on foot. His timing worked out well since those in the crowded streets were less likely to recognize him. However, he was careful to keep his umbrella open to hide his face, since there were many from the town who knew him. Just before entering Lexington, he turned off into a field to lie down under a tree waiting for evening to come.

As darkness approached, Lewis decided to begin walking toward the city. Without being noticed, he went to the washhouse (a separate building on the plantation to wash clothes, iron, etc.) of a man with whom Cyrus used to live. He was pleased that the old slave was there and asked him about Cyrus. The man replied that he was at home and told a young boy in the room to find Cyrus. The man did not recognize Lewis at first. After a couple of moments, he became aware that it was Lewis and exclaimed, "Good heaven, boy! What you back here for? What on earth are you here for, my son? O, I'm scared for you. They will kill you as sure as I'm alive if they catch you! Why in the name of liberty didn't you stay away? I certainly didn't expect to see you again!" Clarke exclaimed, "Don't be scared."

But the old man kept repeating, "I scared for you! I scared for you!"

When Clarke told him why he was in Lexington, he settled down a bit, but he kept repeating, "What brought you back here?"

After a few minutes, Cyrus arrived and was a little less astonished than the old man to see Lewis. Cyrus was told by Lewis approximately a year before when he left Lexington that he would come back for him if he were successful in his attempt to escape. Lewis's promise came true, and Cyrus was overjoyed to see his older brother. He immediately started talking with Lewis about plans for his own escape. Cyrus went back home to his wife, Martha, to tell her about Lewis and to prepare a room for Lewis. Cyrus's wife was a very industrious woman, and because she was free, they were able to rent a comfortable house with a room in the attic where Lewis could be safely concealed.[57]

Cyrus returned and said everything was ready. Lewis went home with him around ten o'clock in the evening. Lewis was stowed away in a little room in the attic that he called his "prison house" for approximately a week. He was unable to move around much but made a point of walking around outside in the evening to exercise. During the day, Cyrus was busy making arrangements for his departure. Cyrus needed the funds that the foremen of various business operations owed him. He was able to retrieve twenty dollars of his money. However, in order not to raise suspicions, he incurred small debts at several establishments, hoping it would deflect any thought that he was fleeing.

Cyrus was not accustomed to walking and proposed that he and Lewis take a couple of horses with them. Lewis objected because if they were caught, they would be accused of horse theft, which would be far worse than running away. Lewis insisted that they travel on foot. They were ready to begin their journey. A family lived in the same house with Cyrus in a room below. The question was how to get out in the early part of the evening without being discovered. Finally they agreed that Cyrus would engage the family in conversation while Lewis slipped out with his bundle of clothes, and they would meet on a pre-designated street corner. As Lewis passed silently out the door, Cyrus was cracking his best jokes with the family and had everyone laughing. This was enough to cover Lewis's retreat. As the frivolity died down, Cyrus excused himself from the family and prepared to join Lewis. By eight o'clock, they were outside the city limits of Lexington. Martha remained at home. After she felt assured Cyrus and Lewis were a safe distance away, she went to the home of Cyrus's master, Dean Logan, pretending distress, and asked if he had seen Cyrus. Her ruse worked. Logan did not suspect her of being involved with the disappearance of her husband. She then began packing her belongings for her journey north to join Cyrus.[58]

When Lewis entered Lexington days earlier, he was so concerned about covering up his face that he did little to notice the roads. On their way out of Lexington, they were perplexed about what roads to take. The moon was bright and the sky clear, but their road to freedom continued to be difficult. At one point, they lifted a signpost out of the ground to read more closely its words, to no avail. As they started off again, Lewis observed that they had not put the signpost back in place. Cyrus smiled, saying he would do that when they came back. Lewis acknowledged that they have never been back to see if it was up or down. Soon after leaving the city, they met many slave patrols but luckily were never questioned by them.

While continuing on by moonlight and often in great doubt about the road, Cyrus was becoming greatly discouraged. He was certain that danger was imminent. The following morning, they were embarrassed, realizing that they had only traveled twenty-five miles. They were elated, however, knowing they were moving in the right direction. Rain had started, and the roads became muddy and slippery. They had not slept the night before and were still very on edge and nervous. In this state of mind, they stopped in a Little patch of bushes to discuss taking a chance to go to a house they saw in a distance to spend the night.

As they sat, Cyrus became very excited and pointed across the road shouting, "Don't you see that animal there?" Lewis looked and saw nothing, but Cyrus affirmed that he saw a dreadful, ugly animal looking at them, ready to spring. Cyrus began to feel for his pistols, but Lewis told him not to fire, but he "continued to point at the imaginary creature." Lewis recalled that he had some hesitation about telling this story because people would not believe him. An acquaintance he knew suggested that such things are not uncommon when the imagination goes awry.[59]

In traveling through the rain and mud that afternoon, they suffered "beyond all power of description." Sometimes they found themselves standing in the middle of the road almost fast asleep. Their feet were completely blistered. When Cyrus got too discouraged, Lewis would urge him on saying they were "walking for freedom now." Half asleep, Cyrus would reply, "Yes, freedom is good, Lewis, but this is a *hard, h-a-r-d* way to get it." They were so weak before night that several times they fell upon their knees in the middle of the road. They had crackers with them, but they had no appetite to eat. Lewis succeeded in convincing Cyrus to go to a house for a night. The good farmer of the home began talking about a large camp meeting taking place two miles from his farm. He complained that group of young men attending were behaving badly by mocking the preachers and disrupting the programs. The supposition was that Lewis and Cyrus were going to the meeting. After sleeping overnight at the farmer's home, they went by the meeting—since it was on their way to Ohio—picked up some gingerbread, and continued to the river. When anyone asked why they were leaving the meeting so soon, they said, "The young men behave so badly, we cannot get any benefit from the meeting."[60]

At eleven o'clock that morning, they reached the river, two miles below Ripley, Ohio. The boatman was on the other side, and they called for him. They tried to be nonchalant, asking questions about the boats as if they were there before. Lewis went to Cyrus and said, "Sir, I have no change, will you lend me enough to pay my toll? I will pay you before we part." When they landed on the northern side of the river, they took a few steps, and Cyrus stopped suddenly, and seeing the water pouring out of the side of the hill, said, "Lewis, give me that tin cup."

"What in the world do you want with a tin cup now? We do not have time to stop." Lewis gave him the cup, and he kept dipping it in the water. Lewis asked him again what he was doing, and Cyrus replied, "This is the first time I ever had a chance to drink water out of *free* dirt." He went a little further and sat on a log and said, "I must sit on this *free* log for a while." Next, he rolled over and over on the ground and exclaimed, "First time I ever rolled on *free* grass." Cyrus continued his ecstatic behavior "as if he were a young and spry colt."[61]

After Cyrus's frolicking subsided, the brothers went up to the house of a good friend of a slave at Ripley. The lady showed them a good bedroom for them to rest. Cyrus was wary. He could not believe anyone could treat him so well. Cyrus exclaimed that she was too good and that they would be captured soon. Cyrus finally settled down as he became more acquainted with the lady and her friends. From the Ripley home, they were escorted by their new friends to several places until they reached Oberlin.

The dangerous mission totaled five weeks from the time Lewis left Oberlin and returned with his youngest brother, Cyrus. Lewis looked back on the horrific rescue of Cyrus, saying to himself, "I had encountered a good deal of peril, had suffered much from anxiety of feeling, but felt richly repaid in seeing another brother free." Lewis and Cyrus stopped in Oberlin for a few days, and then Cyrus continued on to Canada. Even on "free soil," he did not feel particularly safe. His fear was justified. When he reached Lake Erie, he met a man, a Mr. Putnam, who knew him well. Indeed it was the man from whom his wife rented her home in Lexington. The man asked if he was free. He told him yes, he was free, and he was looking for his brother Milton to get him back to Kentucky and settle with old man Archibald Logan for his freedom. Putnam was pleased with Cyrus's response. Putnam continued in his attempt to bait Cyrus with questions. He went on to ask if Cyrus wanted the house where his wife, Martha, lived, and Cyrus replied, "Oh yes, we will notify you when we do not want it anymore. You tell them I shall be down there in a few days. I have heard from Milton and expect to have him soon to carry back with me." Putnam went home and found out what a fool Cyrus made of him. He was embarrassed at being outwitted by a slave.[62]

Cyrus hastened over Lake Erie to Canada; however, he did not like the country as well as the United States and within a few weeks returned and sent a letter to Martha advising her of his safety. He then joined his wife in Hamilton, New York, where they had arranged to meet. Hamilton became their home for many years.

In September of 1842, Lewis and Milton reconnected in Oberlin. Soon after Lewis arrived, at the request of local abolitionists, they left Oberlin and traveled to Madison, Lake County, Ohio, to spend a few days speaking before antislavery audiences. Word of the exploits of the brothers began to gain considerable attention. Milton rode in a carriage to Madison, and Lewis took a stagecoach. Since the brothers had separate schedules for the meetings, it made sense for them to travel separately. The first evening, Milton and Lewis were the guests of a Mr. Philander Winchester, a well-known Ohio abolitionist. They went to a meeting with Mr. Winchester's family on Sunday and in the evening gave an account of their sufferings while in slavery.

Monday morning, Milton and Lewis, with two of Mr. Winchester's family, rode to a Dr. Merriam's home to see the sick daughter of a friend of the brothers'. Milton sat in the carriage for a few moments, and the sick girl and a child of Dr. Merriam came out of the house and asked Milton for a ride. Milton had driven only a mile or so when another carriage came close to him and turned directly across the road in front of his carriage. Several men jumped out and stopped Milton's horse.

He had no idea who they were and asked what they wanted. Milton added that he had half a dollar and would give it to them. One replied, "We do not want your money, but you!" The truth then flashed in Milton's mind: *They are kidnappers!* They surrounded the buggy and ordered him to get out, as one said, "We will have you dead or alive." Milton jumped from the carriage, attempting to run away. He slipped and fell. Immediately four men were on top of him, pushed his head on the ground, and tied up his hands and feet with a rope. The horse, which Milton left on the road, upset the carriage, and the girls were tipped out. Milton implored them to take care of the little girls, who were screaming uncontrollably. One replied, "If you do not hold your tongue, I will cut your damned throats." [63]

Milton was forced into the men's carriage and brought before Associate Judge Page of Centreville, Ohio, on the outskirts of Cincinnati. While on the road, Milton saw a man he knew and told him to take care of the girls in the buggy and to tell Lewis that the kidnappers from Kentucky had caught him. Milton's plea resulted in a kidnapper beating him on the head. One of the captors threatened, "Now we have got you. . . you are the chap that has enticed away so many slaves, we will take care of you, we will have Lewis soon." Milton went before Judge Page. The lead slave catchers were identified as George Postlewaite and Thomas Megowen, who were employed by Deacon Logan as well as other slaveholders in Kentucky. The sheriff of the county, who was sympathetic to the plight of Milton, was present at the proceedings. He asked Milton, "Have you murdered anybody?" He said no. "Have you been stealing?" "No, sir." "What have you done?" Milton said, "Nothing, sir." The sheriff continued, "Why have they tied you up?" Postlewaite interrupted the sheriff's questioning and told him it was none of his business. The sheriff retorted, "Yes, it is my business, and if he has committed no crime, you must untie him."

The sheriff then began to untie Milton. Seeing this, Postlewaite immediately drew his pistols. Judge Page sided with Postlewaite and told the sheriff that he better not touch the gentleman's *property*. The sheriff responded, "We shall see whose property he is." By this time the word spread about Milton's capture, and a large crowd sympathetic to him began to gather around the tavern where the proceedings were held. The slave catchers were represented by Attorney Bob Harper. Clarke's counsel was Salmon P. Chase, who, at the time, was a city councilman from the abolitionist hotbed of Cincinnati, Ohio.[64] In future years he served as Secretary of Treasury in President Lincoln's cabinet and, afterward, Chief Justice of the US Supreme Court.[65] Judge Page ruled in favor of Postlewaite and McGowen as a result of so many letters from prominent Kentuckians, including US Senator Henry Clay, in support of allowing them to take custody of Milton. The judge also sarcastically instructed Milton to "return to his diet of coffee, bread, and butter" on Logan's plantation, which Milton denied ever receiving.

Fearing the crowd gathering at the tavern, the bounty hunters grabbed Milton, drew their pistols, and warned the people not to hinder their arrest. The pistols did not intimidate the citizens. Postlewaite and Megowen were surrounded by the crowd, apprehended, and charged with assault. The crowd worked fast and obtained two writs, one from Lake County to arrest Postlewaite and Megowen as kidnappers and another from Ashtabula county to "take the body" (habeas corpus) of

Milton Clarke. The captors, as well as Milton, were taken by carriage before a magistrate in the town of Unionville on the border of Lake and Ashtabula counties. As the carriage crossed the county line into Ashtabula, the county sheriff stopped the carriage and asked for Milton.

Meanwhile the crowd, most of whom supported Milton's cause, unhitched the horses and surrounded the carriage where the captors and Milton were sitting. A six-foot-tall blacksmith, who at first supported the slave catchers, said, he "wanted no niggers here." Some of Milton's friends asked the blacksmith to point out the "nigger" in the carriage; looking in the carriage for a minute or so, the blacksmith pointed to Postlewaite. Postlewaite angrily replied that any man that calls him a nigger will not go unpunished. The blacksmith insisted that Postlewaite was the nigger. Postlewaite denied the blacksmith's accusation three times. The blacksmith then slapped Postlewaite, who then drew his Bowie knife. The blacksmith picked up a fence rail and began beating the carriage while the crowd was being whipped into fervor. Judge Page became frightened and told Milton to get out of the carriage and added, "The crowd will kill us if you do not get out." At that point the ropes were cut from Milton and he was set free.

The sympathetic sheriff of the county soon lost all knowledge of Milton's whereabouts. The flustered bondsmen were sent back south while their lawyer attempted to console them as they raved and threatened to sue all of northern Ohio.[66] Milton, taking precautions of the likelihood that the slave catchers were continuing to look for him, concealed himself at Austin's farm north of the town of Austinburg. Lewis, evidently, received Milton's warning after his capture, and remained hidden during Milton's legal proceedings.

Subsequent to the furor, the citizens of Austinburg called a meeting together, asking Milton and Lewis to present a lecture on the subject of slavery. No doubt, they had a full house.

A newspaper reporter from the weekly antislavery journal *The Philanthropist* located in Cincinnati covered the incident. The reporter's name was Franklin. It was the pseudonym for Harriet Beecher Stowe who wrote many articles for the *Philanthropist* under that moniker. By becoming Franklin, she enjoyed the voice she was technically denied. "Only white, propertied males had full civil rights. Any single woman who appeared too bright tended to be passed over for marriage by those who were more decorous, discreet and undemonstrative." Hence she chose not to use her true name. [67] This revelation also indicated that Stowe had detailed information about Lewis Clarke and his brother years before Lewis met her in Cambridgeport. Additionally, abolitionist Lewis Tappan, a New York financier and a financial backer of the *Philanthropist,* was certainly aware of Lewis's ventures. He, along with James Birney and Gamaliel Bailey, the editors, saw the potential benefits for the abolitionist movement by promoting Clarke and his stories.

The bounty hunter experience convinced Lewis and Milton that moving to the Northeast could prove to be beneficial and certainly less dangerous. Milton moved to Cambridgeport (Cambridge), Massachusetts, where he lived the remainder of his life. [68] Lewis decided to go to New York City at the behest of Tappan. Lewis was initially introduced to Tappan by R. E. Gillette a merchant in Oberlin. Tappan was also a founder of the American Anti-Slavery Society as well as the American Foreign Anti-Slavery Society. When Clarke arrived in New York, he brought additional laudatory letters from Ohio certifying his experiences. Those who wrote the letters were friends of Tappan, through his association with Oberlin College as well as the antislavery movement in Ohio. After arriving in New York City, Lewis resided in the home of Tappan and eventually moved on to Massachusetts. An interesting and unique relationship was just beginning between the distinguished abolitionist and the fugitive slave from Madison County, Kentucky.

By the end of 1842 Lewis, Cyrus and Milton became free by escaping Kentucky. In Lewis's 1845 *Narrative,* he described the status of his other siblings. Their oldest brother Archy purchased his freedom with the help of the well-known Kentucky abolitionist Cassius Marcellus Clay. Archy repaid Clay, but died seven years later, leaving his wife and three children in slavery. Christiana married a free black and had seven children by him. Her husband was driven away by her master never to be seen again. Dennis was assisted by two whites to gain his freedom and became a successful business man. Alexander, the slave of a Dr. Anderson had an easy time as a slave and had no intention of running away. Sister Delia's short life of sorrow and redemption was described earlier. Manda died at the age of 15 and one other child of their mother died at birth.

Chapter 2

A Call North Amidst
A Movement In Transition

A few years before Lewis Clarke arrived in New York, a major split occurred within the antislavery movement between the New York/Ohio and Massachusetts factions of American Anti-Slavery Society. The separation affected the path Lewis would take within the movement until the beginning of the Civil War. A discussion of the philosophical and political factors that led to the split will provide a better understanding of Clarke's mind-set as an abolitionist during the next twenty years of his life.

From the beginning of the Republic, considerable debate about the institution of slavery was common among national leaders within clerical and political circles. However a serious and recognizable abolitionist movement had not evolved in the United States until the 1830s. In December of 1833, sixty-two abolitionists gathered in Philadelphia to form the American Anti-Slavery Society. (AASS) The focus of the national organization was devoted primarily to immediate emancipation.[69] Those in attendance at the meeting included a cross section of those who would lead the movement for almost three decades. Wealthy Lewis and Arthur Tappan and Reverend Joshua Leavitt were the leading examples of who spoke for socially respectable and committed evangelicals of the New York contingent. Publisher James Birney and cleric Theodore Weld, among other evangelicals, came from Ohio. All philosophically identified with Lewis Tappan and his brother

Arthur. William Lloyd Garrison headed a mixed group of Boston Congregationalists like Samuel E. Sewall, Unitarians such as Samuel May and Quakers like John Greenleaf. Garrison was unquestionably the leader of the latter group. Four Quaker women as well as three black men were among the sixty-two abolitionists who signed the Society's *Declaration of Sentiments.*

Garrison dominated the proceedings in Philadelphia. He gained much of his credibility as the publisher of the Boston newspaper the *Liberator,* which first appeared in 1831. The *Liberator's* attacks on colonization of black slaves, the immediate emancipation of slaves, and its willingness to open its columns to blacks were powerful statements of commitment to the movement. Blacks throughout the Northeast were supportive, initially, of the leadership of Garrison.[70]

Garrison was the primary author of the American Anti-Slavery Society's Declaration of Sentiments. Besides demanding immediate emancipation, the document endorsed nonviolence and firmly rejected "the use of carnal weapons" by abolitionists and slaves. The most challenging portion of the Declaration that the signors pledged was to oppose all racial prejudice wherever it appeared. Garrison himself had difficulty living up to this commitment. The delegates also "pledged to begin organizing antislavery societies in every city town and village and hoped to purify the churches."[71] Lewis and Arthur Tappan held high positions within the new organization and were also the wealthiest. Arthur was named the president of the Society. All members of the Executive Committee, except for one, were New York City residents. The New York City focal point was a business necessity because of the difficulty traveling to and from different areas of the country. Additionally the city was the headquarters for most of the national benevolent societies. The only member of the Executive Committee not from New York was William Lloyd Garrison, the Society's secretary for foreign correspondence.

Early indications of conflict between the New York and Boston factions emerged between Garrison and Arthur Tappan. Arthur, being a very detailed and successful businessman, became concerned about Garrison's haphazard management of his finances. Additionally, Arthur became wary of Garrison's editorial style within the Society's newspaper, the *Liberator,* which alienated his conservative religious acquaintances. Garrison, on the other hand, complained about the Executive

Committee's leadership, feeling that he was battling slavery by himself. Conservative abolitionists such as Lyman Beecher, Harriet Beecher Stowe's father, ridiculed Garrison for "making it impossible for 'decent' people to accept the movement." He suggested, "Get rid of Garrison and thousands will join."[72] Beecher's complaint made no impact on Lewis Tappan at first but Beecher's leadership at Lane Seminary in Cincinnati aggravated Tappan. He and his brother were especially dismayed with Beecher's advocating for the colonization of blacks, which was an anathema to the AASS. A revolt by anticolonization students and faculty at Lane ultimately led to the establishment of Oberlin College in Ohio, the first college in America to accept blacks and women. The Tappan's supported the Lane Rebels. Lewis Tappan exclaimed, "As long as Beecher and his friends call slavery a 'wrong' thing and dare not stigmatize it as a 'sin,' their adhesion would sink us [the movement] to the bottom."[73] Both Tappan brothers, ultimately, became thoroughly disillusioned with Beecher. Tiring of the bickering within the Society led Arthur Tappan to take more interest in Oberlin College than any other project during his involvement within the antislavery movement. His influence helped Oberlin to become the center of Western abolitionism. He soon lost interest in his role as president of the American Anti-Slavery Society, with his brother Lewis filling the void.

In the fall of 1834, evangelicals also began to see serious differences between the abolitionism of Boston and that of New York. One Boston religious journal noted Garrison's "reckless disregard of the courtesies of life and the precepts of Christianity . . ." Garrison was becoming increasingly critical of orthodox Calvinists of New England, and his attacks on slaveholders threatened hope, by the conservatives, of a gradual spread of antislavery principles among Christians in the South. Lewis Tappan, contrary to his brother Arthur's position, opposed the timidity of his business-oriented colleagues serving on the Society's Executive Committee. Lewis grumbled to Garrison, "If the cause [against slavery] is to advance . . . a bold stand should be taken . . . here in Philadelphia and Boston."[74]

Although Garrisonianism had a strong ethical and moral base, the philosophy lacked political and pragmatic relevance for the times. Garrison's followers claimed that churches and the US government obstructed progress toward absolute parity toward abolitionism and its varied forms. They denounced all aspects of coercion and military measures including carrying a rifle, capital punishment, and jail. In essence, Garrison's philosophy was a rejection of history and a rebellion against religious traditionalism. The doctrine ultimately denounced the US Constitution and later demanded for a northern union, politically and morally separated from the values of the Southern states. Garrisonianism remained true to its commitment to nonresistance, which was later challenged by the radical abolitionists of the 1850s.[75]

A major change within the antislavery winds came from the Massachusetts orthodox Calvinist clergy in June of 1837. Nehemiah Adams, a well-known Congregational minister, and several other clergy met and wrote a pastoral letter that was distributed and read in many pulpits during the middle of July. The letter deplored Garrisonian agitation, which encouraged disrespect of the clerical office and disapproved of "unnatural" presumptions of advocates of women's rights. The letter was followed by publications of two pastors who had a limited connection with the American Anti-Slavery Society, called *The Appeal of Clerical Abolitionists and Anti-Slavery Measures* and three other appeals from prominent clergy throughout the Northeast. All the appeals were challenges to Garrison's leadership. Garrison retaliated by condemning the nation's clergy as "blind leaders of the blind, dumb dogs that cannot bark, spiritual popes—that. . . love the fleece better than the flock."[76]

The split between the New York and Boston factions of the Society continued to grow. Writing Lewis Tappan, his friend in past disputes with the New York committee, Garrison asked, "Does it indeed not concern the Parent Society, that five clergymen, professed abolitionists, have publicly impeached. . . its 'leading' advocates?"[77] Tappan replied to Garrison in a friendly but evasive way, essentially pointing out that the Executive Committee was too busy to become the arbiter for personal and local affairs. Clearly Garrison was offensive to the local leaders. The Tappan's felt for the Committee to reject them was to reject the rank and file of the American Anti-Slavery Society.[78] Garrison concluded that the New Yorkers "would be glad, on the whole to see me cashiered or voluntarily leave the ranks." His assessment was correct. As events unfolded, he was justified in extending his attack on the leadership of the Society. They were unimaginative and locked up in administrative detail. Garrison was justifiably fed up with the slow-moving Executive

Committee. However, the Committee became energized by their dismay of Garrison. While publically remaining neutral, they prepared to take action to free antislavery doctrine from Garrison's "heresies" about war, women, and social institutions. The Committee was slowly being driven into the arms of the liberal-talking, well-meaning protectors of the existing order. However, the Boston faction of the movement had more strength than Tappan imagined.

During 1838 and 1839, the intrigues expanded steadily. Lewis Tappan and the Society's Executive Committee gradually lost control over the situation. Tappan, anticipating strong turns of events in favor of Garrison's Boston contingent, spent most of 1839 and early 1840 dismantling the old Anti-Slavery Society. Tappan became aware of the British Anti-Slavery Society, formed in 1839, and liked the direction it was moving. The focus of the new organization was to revive their nation's floundering antislavery cause. Tappan considered the British approach as an excellent model for a new association once the evangelicals departed from the old Society. Last-minute, half-hearted efforts to resuscitate the Society failed to rally the support of the Central Committee. Garrison's followers were overjoyed by the muddle in New York, calling the national officers "incompetent." They were ready to take control as soon as the opportunity permitted. Tappan supporters prepared for the worst.

On May 11, 1840, over one thousand abolitionists attended the AASS convention at the Fourth Avenue Free Church in New York. Arthur failed to appear to preside but sent a letter of resignation. Brother Lewis chaired the meeting in his absence, attempting to give his New York faction the impression of fighting for the Executive Committee down to the wire. Events moved quickly with Garrison's associate, Frances Jackson, elected to fill the vacated chair by Arthur Tappan. Garrison's slate of candidates won most of the seats on the Executive Committee. Garrison generously recommended Lewis Tappan for a place on the reconstituted Committee. However, Garrison also nominated a woman, Abbey Kelly, a fiery feminist. Kelly won the vote amid cheers by Garrison's supporters. Tappan immediately gave four reasons gentlemen should not sit behind closed doors with women and abruptly resigned from the Committee.[79]

That evening thirty leaders gathered with Lewis Tappan at his home where he read to them a constitution he had drafted some weeks before. The gathering adopted it, forming the American and Foreign Anti-Slavery Society and elected Lewis as its president. Missing from the gathering were some of Tappan's most loyal supporters. They included true luminaries within the antislavery circles—Gerrit Smith, Alvan Stewart, Elizur Wright, the Grimkes, and Theodore Weld. The vision of the new group was to foster international accord on slavery matters; however, the concept was too broad and vague to have a meaningful impact on American slavery to arouse significant interest.

Garrison's cadre of abolitionists remained small but continued to be very vocal. The public mind always associated the Society with William Lloyd Garrison, not its national officers. Probably Tappan's most important contribution to political antislavery, which Garrison eschewed, was the founding of the Washington *National Era,* under the editorship of Gamiel Bailey, Tappan's choice for the position. Tappan organized the fundraising for Bailey's salary and the paper's operation until it was self-sustaining. Its first issue appeared on January 7, 1847. The paper served very effectively as the Liberty Party's most well-known journal. The *Era* was also utilized as the springboard for the popularity of author Harriet Beecher Stowe's *Uncle Tom's Cabin.* The story was serialized in the *National Era,* prior to the book's publication in 1852.[80]

Lewis Clarke's decision to accept Lewis Tappan's invitation to move to the Northeast is understandable. The Ohio faction of the American Anti-Slavery Society was well connected with the Tappan brothers and prominent Ohio abolitionists prior to Lewis moving east. After Lewis came back from Canada to Ohio in search of Milton, Tappan's Oberlin abolitionist friends immediately befriended Clarke and convinced him to speak to abolitionist sympathizers in and around Oberlin about his experiences as a slave. Ohio abolitionists also rescued his brother Milton from being captured by Kentucky slave bounty hunters in early 1842. Clarke was never known to voice adherence to the antislavery agenda of William Lloyd Garrison, who was against the utilization of military resistance and capital punishment and denunciated the "immoral" US Constitution and the Declaration of Independence. Clarke was proud that his father and grandfather had fought against suppression during the Revolutionary War. Contrary to Garrison, Clarke considered the full adherence to the Declaration of Independence and the Constitution as the vehicles for ultimate freedom for blacks in America. Nonresistance was not part of Clarke's makeup. Clarke also carried weapons most of his life and intended to use them if necessary. Essentially, Clarke could relate readily to what he considered the more practical antislavery principles advocated by Lewis Tappan.

Soon after Clarke arrived in New York City, Lewis Tappan sent a note to Lydia Maria Child informing her that a fugitive slave [Clarke] nearly as white as himself would address an audience in Brooklyn and suggested that it would be to her benefit to hear his story. At the time, Child was the editor of the *Anti-Slavery Standard* and previously connected with Tappan as a member of the American Anti-Slavery Society. The Brooklyn meeting took place on October 20, 1842. Child related her impressions of Clarke's speech in her famous article "Leaves from a Slave's Journal of Life."[81] Child exclaimed, "I have seldom been more entertained by any speaker . . . few who heard him went away without being impressed by the conviction that he was sincerely truthful."

Child said Tappan introduced Clarke to the gathering, saying that he brought highly recommended letters from Ohio including a "Judge King, and General Somebody and Esquire Somebody." The letters certified the truthfulness of Clarke's story. Child claimed she did not remember their names, because she did not revere great "names." She felt Tappan was "propping up his protégé" with the influential names when it was not necessary to do so. The audience, she said, could hear that Clarke spoke the truth from *what* he said and the *way* he said it and did not need the aide of the generals and judges. Child's comments were a clear indication of the tension between the followers of Tappan and Garrison. Child remained a strong follower of the Garrisonians, not the Tappans of New York and Ohio. The letters supporting Clarke were from stellar Ohio abolitionists such as former Revolutionary War General Edward Paine; future Chief Justice of the United States Supreme Court, Solomon Chase, Esquire; and the Honorable J. R. Giddings, a member of the United States House of Representatives.

Clarke lectured the Brooklyn audience for three consecutive evenings. He had not learned to read or write at that point in his life and, from time to time, had difficulty finding the correct word to express his ideas during the lectures. Child praised Clarke by saying he was naturally intelligent and that his remarks were "valuable for their honest directness and simplicity." She lamented, "What might have been, with common advantages for education, is shown by his shrewd conclusions, and the large ideas which his soul struggles so hard to utter in imperfect language." Child was speaking about Clarke intimating that his lack of education doomed him forever. Clarke was only twenty-seven when spoke to the Brooklyn audience. His life was just beginning. The fact that the young Clarke had the charisma and intelligence to hold the attention of the large crowds for days was a significant testament of his innate attributes as a speaker, although he never became the orator on the scale of his colleague Frederick Douglass. Clarke described a variety of the horrors he personally suffered or witnessed as a slave. However, he wanted his audience to realize that being whipped, beaten, and not having enough to eat, although terrible, were not the worst aspects of slavery. In anguish, Clarke pleaded, "But what I want you to understand is that *a slave can't be a man*! Slavery makes a brute of man." Child said naively, "I was very much struck with the fact the he [Clarke] seemed to think much less of the physical sufferings of the slave, than of his moral and intellectual degradation." Some revisionists of American history contend that slavery was not as bad as portrayed by Clarke. Others refuse to talk about the "peculiar institution" as if it never happened. Clarke's stories remind us that we need not dwell on the horrors of slavery; however, by not recognizing how its remnants affect American society today, it will clearly limit our ability to achieve true equal opportunity for African Americans.

Clarke's most profound observation in his Brooklyn speech came from this statement: "My grandmother was her master's daughter, and my mother was her master's daughter, and I was my master's son, so you see I haven't got but one eighth of the [black] blood. Now, admitting its right to make a slave of a full black nigger, I want to ask gentlemen acquainted with the business whether because I owe a shilling, I ought to be made to pay a dollar?" Clarke was never ashamed of his black blood; nevertheless, his riveting question made abundantly clear the irrational, greedy, and racist basis of the "one-drop rule." None of the businessmen in the audience responded to Lewis's challenge. However, it is interesting to note when the American slave trade ended with the Slave Trade Act of 1807, there were approximately 890,000 slaves in America, and by 1830, the slave population more than doubled to over two million. Was a factor of the tremendous increase in the slave population, without the slave trade, due to greater application of the one-drop rule? Certainly with the invention of the cotton gin, presumably, by Eli Whitney in 1793, which separated seeds from raw cotton, the supply and demand of cotton increased, which in turn required greater numbers of slaves. As Clarke's story attests, the slave masters were doing their part for the cotton economy through miscegenation, to ensure that they did not have to depend upon the slave trade. Lust aside, the one-drop rule was, at the least, a good business decision for the slave masters, although it was a deal with the devil.

Clarke's point continues to be debated today among blacks and whites as to what constitutes race. Biologists unequivocally agree that racial categories have no biological reality. However, Clarke was of the opinion that the one-drop rule, although fashioned out of ignorance and greed, united a people who could be proud of their customs and heritage as well as fight against slavery and racial injustice.[82] At the end of Clarke's marathon presentation, Tappan told Ms. Child that a slave owner from Mississippi was in attendance who said afterward that he heard nothing he considered noncredible from Clarke. He said he was going to emancipate his slaves "forthwith." Tappan added, "God give him the grace to keep his word."[83] Soon after Clarke's triumphant appearance in Brooklyn, he moved on to reside in Cambridgeport, Massachusetts, where his brother had moved months earlier.

Both brothers became active in abolitionist causes and lectured throughout New England, with Lewis being more involved than his brother. While in Cambridgeport, Lewis began a seven-year residence with Aaron Safford, a Boston merchant, and his wife Mary, stepdaughter of Lyman Beecher, Harriet Beecher Stowe's father. Mary H. Jackson Safford was the daughter of Lyman Beecher's third wife, Lydia Beals Jackson. Clarke never gave specifics on how he became a resident of the Safford home. However, there is no doubt that Tappan, as his mentor, arranged for him to live with the Saffords, who were solid standard-bearers for the movement. Harriet Beecher Stowe was likely involved in placing Lewis with her sister-in-law, having written the 1842 *Philanthropist* article about the Clarkes and their dangerous and exciting confrontation with the slave catchers in Oberlin, only months before Lewis's arrival in Cambridgeport.

In December 1842, Lewis met Reverend Joseph C. Lovejoy in Cambridgeport, to whom Lewis dictated his 1845 *Narrative of the Sufferings of Lewis Clarke: During a Captivity of More Than Twenty-Five*

Years among the Algerines of Kentucky, One of the So-Called Christian States of North America, Dictated by Himself. Reverend Lovejoy, a Congregational pastor, was also an activist in the abolitionist movement. His more famous brother, Elijah Lovejoy, was killed by an anti-abolitionist mob in Alton, Illinois, in 1837 while defending his antislavery printing press. Elijah was an ally of Harriet Beecher Stowe's older brother Edward Beecher. Clarke met Joseph Lovejoy through Lewis Tappan who hired him and his brother Owen in 1838 to write what became a widely acclaimed memoir of his brother Elijah. During that year, Joseph worked out of Tappan's International American Anti-Slavery office in New York City.[84]

By 1842 Lewis was a notable figure within the antislavery movement as indicated by numerous newspaper accounts in Kentucky, Ohio, and the Northeast. Lovejoy noted an example of Lewis popularity in the early 1840s when famous abolitionist and wealthy Kentucky planter, Cassius Marcellus Clay, saw Lewis's brother Milton in Boston one day and "recognized him as one of the Clarke family well known to him in Kentucky."[85] Clay was also a close friend of Abraham Lincoln and a founder of the Republican Party.

When Reverend Lovejoy first met Lewis, he was impressed immediately with the fugitive slave's intelligence and integrity. He noted in the preface of Lewis's *Narrative,* "I remember, too, the wave on wave of deep feeling excited in an audience of more than a thousand persons, at Hallowell, Me., as they listened to his story, and looked upon his energetic and manly countenance." Joseph and Tappan persuaded Clarke to dictate his *Narrative,* which he initially published as a pamphlet in 1843 and sold at abolitionist meetings. Many copies of the 1845 hard back edition of his *Narrative* were purchased, but Lewis's graphic descriptions of slavery disturbed so many people throughout New England it resulted in several thousand copies being suppressed and the plates destroyed. Few original copies exist today.[86]

Frederick Douglass also published his slave narrative in 1845, but after Clarke's account. Dr. John Blassingame stated in his Introduction to *Narrative of the Life of Frederick Douglass* that before Douglass published his narrative, "Between 1838 and 1845, he [Douglass] read many antislavery publications . . . that contained speeches, interviews, and autobiographies of dozens of fugitive slaves including Lunsford Lane, James Curry, *Lewis Clarke,* and the *Amistad* rebels."[87]

Milton subsequently dictated his story to Lovejoy, which was added to Lewis's 1845 book. The new 1846 publication was entitled *Narratives of the Sufferings of Lewis and Milton Clarke, Sons of a Soldier of the Revolution, During a Captivity of More Than Twenty Years among the Slaveholders of Kentucky, One of the So-Called Christian States of North America, Dictated by Themselves.* The primary differences between the two stories were the episodes of Delia, their sister, and Milton's confrontation with the slave catchers near Oberlin. Each is written in greater detail within Milton's narrative. The book had brisk sales at abolitionist gatherings throughout the United States "and the young men made some money out of it."[88] The publication of *Uncle Tom's Cabin* in 1852 led to renewed interest in all slave autobiographies, especially those of Josiah "Uncle Tom" Henson, Frederick Douglass, and [Lewis] Clarke.[89] The second book was published because of the brisk sales of Lewis's earlier *Narrative.* The results were positive; however, the exact sales figures are not clear. Milton's estimate of 150,000 being sold over many years may not be an exaggeration since two London firms, Wortley and Chapman Brothers published the stories in 1846.

In referring to the years Lewis lived at the home of Mary and Aaron Safford, Lewis often remarked that Mrs. Safford "taught me more than anyone else." He would also add that Mrs. Safford's daughters would occasionally take on the role of teachers during his stay. While living with the Saffords, Lewis joined the Second Evangelical Congregational Church, pastored by Reverend Lovejoy. The proud Clarke must have been dismayed learning they had to sit in the "Negro pews" of the sanctuary during services. The discriminatory policy was an indication of the incongruity of the abolitionist movement and the kind of experience that Lewis had to face on a regular basis in the "promised land" of the north. The Lovejoy brothers placed their lives on the line against the inhuman institution of slavery, yet Pastor Lovejoy was unable to allow his black and white church members to sit together. Interestingly, a few years after Lewis joined the church, Pastor Lovejoy made a small gesture in an attempt to right the wrong by having a black sit next to his wife in the white section of sanctuary. The pastor was summarily fired by the congregation. Ironically, the firing took place in 1853, a year after the publication of *Uncle Tom's Cabin,* and in the heart of the antislavery movement, Cambridge, Massachusetts. Lovejoy never served as pastor for another church.[90] The bigoted seating arrangement in the church was one of many mixed messages concerning race that gnawed at Lewis during his stay in New England.

The foremost black abolitionist of the day, Frederick Douglass, was a victim of New England's racial climate from Boston's William Lloyd Garrison, the leading spokesman of the antislavery movement. Political differences had been simmering between Douglass and Garrison for years, which degenerated into "vituperative and personal feuding." Their troubles surfaced in May 1851. Douglass shocked Garrison at the annual American Anti-Slavery Society meeting by objecting to a resolution praising the work of abolitionist newspapers. The AASS only endorsed papers that shared the disunionist (i.e., separation of slave and antislave states) credo. Douglass told the gathering that he analyzed the matter and concluded that he could not support the credo and had to disqualify his *North Star* newspaper from the list. He believed that the US Constitution offered no protection to slavery, and he would henceforth advocate political action, including voting, for slavery's abolition. Douglass was taking a position against two basic tenants of Garrisonism: recognition of the legitimacy of the Constitution and participating in the political process. Douglass considered Garrison's position against the political process as impractical. In his mind, the Garrisonians had been wrongheaded, and he declared, "There is no question. . . that the anti-slavery movement will always be followed to a greater or lesser distance by a political party of some sort. It is inevitable."[91] Douglass began to distance himself further from the AASS by advancing a separatist agenda, which included a National Black Council and a black manual training school. Garrison's anger smoldered for a period of time but erupted in September of 1853 when he condemned Douglass as "an artful and unscrupulous schismatic" whose attacks gave fresh ammunition to the proslavery press while assuming the color of his skin would shield him from critics.[92] He went on to warn Douglass not to cast aspersions on "those who have been his friends and to whom he is eternally indebted from emerging from obscurity." Garrison was saying, essentially, that Douglass would be a nonentity if not for him. Garrison's fury went beyond the personal accusations to attacks on the black race: "He railed at the idea that the fugitive slaves possessed superior wisdom. He angrily opined that perhaps the 'sufferers" special circumstances had transcended their ability as a class to understand all that the cause required." As a black man, Douglass did not have the intellect to comprehend the repercussions he would face from the decisions he was making. Almost in disbelief, Douglass responded by saying Garrison's statements were a "stupendous insult comparable to colonizationists' charges of natural inferiority" of blacks. The preciseness of Garrison's words reflected a substratum of racism within the heart and mind of the titular head of the American Anti-Slavery Society. Harriet Beecher Stowe thrust herself into the embarrassing public feud. She contacted each of them, admonishing, "Silence in this case will be eminently *golden.*" Even though Garrison's attacks were more severe and mean-spirited than Douglass's, she was more pointed with the black leader. She lectured that there was ample room within the separate antislavery movements for them to work together. She also held out a "carrot" to Douglass, saying if he worked toward cessation of the public hostilities that she would support the training school for former slaves that he desired. Douglass later on followed up with her on this matter, with embarrassing results. Stowe advised Garrison to be patient with Douglass because he was "still growing" philosophically. She also counseled him by saying, "What Douglas *is* really, time will show." Her statement, though well-intended, came across as viewing Douglass as immature. At the time he was over thirty-five years of age. The public vituperative statements between the two men faded away, but they never came back together on the essential approaches needed to eliminate the institution of slavery. Garrison's race-laden attacks against Douglass certainly did not help matters and must have been etched in his mind. Garrison's outbursts, though disappointing, did not surprise him; however, they underpinned the impressions he had of the north as reflected in his first speech as an abolitionist: "Prejudice against color is stronger north than south; it hangs around my neck like a heavy weight. It presses me out from my fellow men . . . I have met it every step the three years I have been out of slavery."[93] However; Douglass gave Garrison faint praise by stating that he was indebted to Garrison because he plowed the ground to create the Free Soil Party, knowing full well that Garrison was against the anti-slavery movement from becoming involved in politics. The separation between Douglass and Garrison became irreparable when Douglass, Lewis Tappan, Gerrit Smith, and John Brown, among others, founded the Radical Abolitionist Party in Syracuse, New York, in the summer of 1855. Contrary to Garrisonian beliefs, the Radical

Abolitionists supported the Constitution and insisted that slavery had to be removed from every inch of American soil by any means necessary— even violence. [94]

Lewis Clarke had the same perspectives of the racial climate in the Northeast as Douglass, but it did not hinder either of them from continuing their relentless battle against slavery. Although Garrison's fiery style and laudatory oratory skills drew more attention as the voice of the abolitionist movement, Clarke and Douglass concluded that the best approach to eliminate slavery was through the pragmatic political processes advocated by Garrison's rivals such as the Tappan brothers of New York.

Chapter 3

The Phenomenon Of *Uncle Tom's Cabin*

While living with Mary and Aaron Safford in Cambridgeport during the 1840s, Lewis Clarke's notoriety continued to spread with the publication of his two narratives. Additionally, large crowds throughout the Northeast attended his speaking engagements. As Lewis's popularity was rising, Mary Safford arranged for Lewis to meet her sister-in-law, Harriet Beecher Stowe, in 1844, who at the time was an aspiring writer. Their first meeting led to repeated interviews of Lewis in the Safford home over a period of several years. Lewis pointed out that "Mrs. Stowe visited there on purpose to hear my story. She used to send for me to come to the parlor and talk with me for hours at a time about my experiences as a slave."[95] He went on to say that on those occasions she wrote notes of all that he told her and kept them until after the passage of the Fugitive Law in 1850, at which time it became politically prudent to begin writing her novel.[96] Lewis, during his years with the Saffords, was also dictating his *Narrative* to Joseph Lovejoy. It was during the same time frame that Stowe was taking notes from Lewis. Since Stowe and Lovejoy were active in the antislavery movement and connected with the same power brokers, it stands to reason that they compared notes of their conversations with Lewis. Because of their mutual professional interests, it would have been natural for them to do so.

While with the Saffords, Lewis observed that Mrs. Stowe was not as strong on the antislavery cause as Mrs. Safford and yet she was anxious for Lewis to give Stowe as much information as possible because she was a person of considerable influence. [97]Lewis's opinion of Stowe was confirmed by the author herself in a letter to Gamaliel Bailey, publisher of *The New Era* in March of 1851: "*Up until this year* I have always felt that I had no particular call to meddle with this subject [slavery], and I dreaded to expose even my own mind to the full force of its exciting power. But I feel now that the time has come when even a woman or a child who can speak a word for freedom and humanity is bound to speak."[98] Her comments raise the question as to the factor(s) that led her to become more committed to the movement.

The antislavery movement in the Northern states had become divided between the followers of Garrison and the Tappans. Lewis Tappan and Gamiel Bailey, who were the financial backer and editor, respectively, of the abolitionist journal *National Era* became the voice of the politically active Liberty Party. Tappan and Bailey represented the moderate wing of the antislavery movement. As noted previously, the followers of William Lloyd Garrison were more radical and uncompromising on the slavery issue as well as women's suffrage. Tappan, Bailey, and Lewis Tappan's brother Arthur believed that the antislavery cause needed a drastic new direction and formed a rival organization, the American and Foreign Anti-Slavery Society. They, according to Clarke, felt that the little-known mother, wife, and writer Harriet Beecher Stowe embodied the characteristics that would reenergize the movement and therefore garner greater public support. Clearly they did not anticipate the unprecedented results of their change in direction.

Lewis Clarke provided some fascinating recollections he gave to a reporter on how Harriet Beecher Stowe came to write her classic novel:

> Dr. [Gamaliel] Bailey, who published *The Philanthropist* in Cincinnati, had been persuaded by Lewis Tappan to move to Washington City [Washington D. C.] in 1846 where he published *The National Era*.[99] When the fugitive slave law [1850] was passed it produced such an impression upon the country, and was so strongly sustained by the press and even the pulpit, that the emancipationists were paralyzed for some time. *The National Era* lost circulation steadily, and was on the point of extinction, when Dr. Bailey went to New York to consult with some leading emancipationists as to what course he should pursue. He thought he could get

some woman of literary reputation and ability to write a
series of articles for his paper every week on the subject
of slavery and its violation of the finest sentiments, that
it would receive public interest and carry his paper to
people it had never reached before. The names of Lydia
M. Child and others were proposed but not accepted.
Lewis Tappan, who was one of the counselors, finally
said he knew of one woman who could do the work
successfully; that she was poor and must be paid for
it, but that she would succeed. He then mentioned
Mrs. Stowe, and advised Dr. Bailey to write her, and by
way of earnest, inclose [sic] her a draft for $100. The
letter was written and the draft sent. The next week
there appeared in the columns of *The National Era,*
not the first of a series of articles on slavery, but the
first chapters of a story called *Uncle Tom's Cabin.* The
effect was instantaneous and great.[100] Circulation of *The
National Era* was increased at once, and soon became
very large. Mrs. Stowe was poor and earning her money
so laboriously that for fear the great novel would be cut
short she was sent an additional draft for $300. Then
she copyrighted the story, which became more famous
than any novel ever issued from a printing press.[101]

The reporter, who interviewed Clarke, added "Into the book she
wove all the facts given her by Lewis Clarke, in connection with the
information gleaned elsewhere."[102] Assuming the veracity of Clarke's
account, the writing of the great novel was a politically motivated and
clearly orchestrated selection process on the part of abolitionist leaders
with Lewis Tappan at the forefront. Documented history shows that
Tappan played similar roles in other significant events related to the
abolitionist movement. He worked in the background, financially and
otherwise, to establish the groundbreaking race- and gender-integrated
Oberlin College in Ohio. Tappan was also the force behind the scenes
concerning the famous US Supreme Court *Amistad* case of 1839.
Tappan hired the attorneys, including former United States president
John Quincy Adams, to defend the illegally enslaved Africans of the
Spanish slave ship *Amistad.* The slaves, under the leadership of the

brilliant African Cinque, mutinied and killed the captain and crew. The ship sailed from Havana, went off course, and was picked up off Long Island by the USS *Washington* and taken to New Haven. The blacks were arrested and taken to jail. Southern senators insisted that they be tried for murder and conspiracy by a federal court.[103] As a result of Tappan's efforts, the case was won on appeal to the US Supreme Court in 1839, and the slaves were freed. Of all the letters of congratulations that he received regarding the victory, the one he treasured the most was from Adams who declared, "The captives are free! But thanks, thanks in the name of humanity and justice to you."[104] At that point in US history, the case was the most significant concerning slavery until eclipsed by the Dred Scott decision in 1857, which determined unequivocally that Negroes were not citizens of the United States and, as such, had no civil rights.

Clarke was likely in the middle of the machinations with Tappan because he knew most, if not all, of the main players, and his story was powerful grist for the abolitionist mill. Clarke pointed out unabashedly in an 1890 *Washington Post* interview that "if she [Stowe] had not gotten acquainted with me she [Stowe never could have written that book in her life, for she would not have been able to get the information."[105]

Young E. Allison, a highly respected reporter for the *Louisville Courier*, stated that "the book [*Uncle Tom's Cabin*] which Lewis Clarke aided in producing (and nobody who reads his *Narrative* can doubt where Mrs. Stowe got most of her facts and suggestions). . . created a situation where black children in 1881 were learning to read and write in rural Lowell, Kentucky which in all *probability* could not have happened without the publication of the book."[106] Allison was referring to the fact that slave owners did not allow their "property" to read or write.

Harriet Beecher Stowe's novel first appeared in the *National Era* in serial form. The story reflected the moderate and pragmatic message the publishers desired. She portrayed slaves as mostly docile and God-fearing, whose families were decimated by the system. Her story line resonated, particularly with white Northern mothers. The book was also a revelation to white Northerners in that "Negroes" were indeed human beings, not property, and as such deserved to be free.

Stowe's personal background gave her credibility with her Northern target audience. She personified mainstream New England life in that she was a devout Christian, a devoted wife, and the mother of nine children. Additionally, she was not considered an antislavery zealot as her friend William Lloyd Garrison was portrayed by his enemies. Garrison must have been dismayed that Stowe ultimately aligned with Tappan's politically focused *National Era* rather than his *Liberator* publication.

The timing of the publication in 1852 was also important since the Fugitive Slave Law of 1850 made Northerners uncomfortable and even fearful of bands of slave catchers swarming into their communities seeking escaped slaves from the South. There was also fear that the new law and the political climate could lead to slavery being spread to an even greater degree in the Northern states which could lead to scarce jobs available to whites in the north. The picture that Stowe painted of slavery was not what they wanted incorporated within their communities. Moral enlightenment was not necessarily a primary consideration.

The impact of *Uncle Tom's Cabin* on the United States and the world was unprecedented and a "phenomenon in terms of sales and its popularity and influence." The novel became "the world's first blockbuster."[107] In 1853, three hundred thousand copies were sold in the United States and two million around the world.[108]

A year after the publication of the novel, Stowe felt compelled to write another book, entitled *The Key to Uncle Tom's Cabin*. She explained in the first chapter, "At times, doubt has been expressed whether the scenes and characters portrayed in *Uncle Tom's Cabin* convey a fair representation of slavery as it present exists. This work, more perhaps, than any other work of fiction that was written, has been a collection and arrangement of real incidents, of actions really performed, of words and expressions really uttered." She then wrote over five hundred pages that described the real people and incidents indicating that the characters and story line were not figments of her imagination.

As noted, a lead character in her novel was George Harris, the rebellious quadroon slave. Detractors of George complained that the character was "overdrawn, both as respects personal qualities and general intelligence." Naysayers also complained that the incidents George encountered were improbable and reflected a distorted view of the institution of slavery. Stowe in response wrote in the *Key* that Clarke was the primary prototype of George Harris. She went further by describing her personal but strangely oblique connection with Lewis and quoted from large sections of Lewis's *Narrative:*[109]

> Lewis Clark is an acquaintance of the writer. Soon after his escape from slavery, he was received into the family of a sister-in-law of the author, and there educated. His conduct during this time was such as to win for him uncommon affection and respect, and the author has frequently heard him spoken of in the highest terms by all who knew him.
>
> The gentleman in whose family he so long resided, says of him in a recent letter to the writer, "I would trust him, as the saying is, with untold gold."
>
> Lewis is a quadroon, a fine looking man, with European features, hair slightly wavy, and with an intelligent, agreeable expression and countenance. His mother was a handsome quadroon woman, the daughter of her master, and given by him in marriage to a free white man, a Scotchman, with the express understanding that she and her children were to be free. This engagement, if made sincerely at all, was never complied with. His mother had nine children and on the death of her husband, came back, with all these children, as slaves in her father's house.

Stowe then goes on, quoting various scenes directly from Lewis's *Narrative.*

Further in the *Key*, Mrs. Stowe refers to the terrible beating of Delia, the sister of Lewis and Milton: "Milton Clark, a brother of Lewis, in the narrative of his life, describes the scene where he, with his mother stood at the door while this girl was brutally whipped by slave master Joseph Logan for wishing to conform to the principles of her Christian profession."[110]

Why Stowe does not mention Mrs. Safford's name in the *Key* nor is more precise about Lewis's relationship with the Saffords is open to conjecture. Additionally, Stowe's push-pull personal relationship with Lewis was mysterious.

Acclaimed biographer Joan D. Hedrick stated that "it is well known that for her plot [for Uncle Tom's Cabin] Stowe drew upon the narratives of escaped slaves, particularly those of Josiah Henson and Henry Bibb,"[111] without mentioning Lewis Clarke. Stowe's *Key,* as well as research by authorities such as John Blassingame, David Reynolds and Yuval Taylor place in many respects more emphasis on the significance of Clarke regarding the plot. As documented, Clarke met with Stowe on numerous occasions before the writing of *Uncle Tom's Cabin.* Lewis also knew Bibb. His experiences closely resembled Clarke's in that they were both born in Kentucky, their parents were of mixed blood, and they had adventurous stories about bringing relatives out of bondage to freedom in Canada. The extremely bright Bibb, also a gifted orator and writer, was the editor of Canada's first black newspaper in Canada, *The Voice of the Fugitive.* Despite similarities of the lives of Clarke and Bibb, there was no indication in the research that Bibb met Stowe; however, there is evidence that they wrote to each other. Also there is no reference to Bibb at all in Stowe's five-hundred page volume, *The Key to Uncle Tom's Cabin.*

About a year after the publication of *Uncle Tom's Cabin,* Lewis was in Andover, Massachusetts, lecturing on temperance, and related a surprising and curious experience:

> I found that Mrs. Stowe was then a resident of Andover, Massachusetts and one day she sent me a pressing invitation to come to her house and take dinner with her and her family. She met me at the door and was very gracious. She shook hands with me, asked me how I was getting along and introduced me to her children, which [*sic*] were very small.

> I sat at her right at the table and during the meal she talked a great deal about slavery, and asked me if I had read *Uncle Tom's Cabin.* I told her I had and asked her why she did not send for me before she printed the story, as I would have straightened out some things she got wrong.

She replied, "*You slaves* are so reserved that I didn't think you would come if I sent for you. When I was taking notes of your conversation at my sister's I had no idea I would ever use them as I expected to keep them for relics. But when Mr. [Lewis] Tappan and others asked me to write about slavery I found my notes of great value. But you told me then more facts than the people are willing to believe, and I have written another book to tell where I got my information [*The Key to Uncle Tom's Cabin*]."

Clarke replied that he would have quickly responded to her if she had asked and she seemed pleased. Clarke remained at Stowe's Andover home for several hours talking with her and her children. The dinner with Harriet was the last time he saw her. Shortly afterward, he traveled back to Ontario, Canada.[112] Although they never saw each other again, their relationship was far from over.

Research indicates that during the time Lewis and Harriet knew each other, it was she who initiated the contacts. Her interest in Lewis began in 1842 when Stowe, hid behind the "Franklin" pseudonym in the *Philanthropist* newspaper to report on the slave-catcher confrontation involving Lewis and Milton outside of Oberlin. Lewis likely never knew of her coverage of the incident. Again, it was Stowe, along with her sister-in-law Mary Safford, who arranged for Lewis to meet with the author on numerous occasions to inquire about Lewis's life story. Then, out of the blue, a few years later when Lewis was visiting Andover, Stowe found out that he was in town and sent him a note asking him to have an evening dinner with her.

The meetings of Lewis and Mrs. Stowe in Cambridgeport and Andover were daring considering the Victorian mores of the times. Conservative New Englanders would not approve of a single man, much less a black man, meeting alone with a married white woman. This writer has never found, through his research, any reference attributed to Stowe that these meetings took place. Was Stowe covering up the information because of concern about the implications of the meetings?

There are no indications that Lewis ever sought any remuneration from Stowe for the story lines he provided for her book, although he was more than justified to do so. He never spoke publicly against Stowe about the slight. However, soon after the dinner with Stowe in Andover, he contacted her by letter asking for a reference statement. He did not mention money. He asked her for a letter saying he had given her some of the incidents of her book, nothing else. Although Stowe acknowledged that he did give her such information, Stowe indignantly declined to "render him that poor service." Deeply hurt, Clarke merely said, "For all Mrs. Stowe's writing so much against slavery and slave holders, my young master, Tom Kennedy, wouldn't have treated a dog like that."[113] Lewis's seething anger exudes from his remarks by comparing one of the nation's leading advocates against slavery to a slave master. Lewis merely asked for a note from Stowe to put in writing what she had already written in *The Key to Uncle Tom's Cabin*. He never ever asked her for another favor.

A variety of concerns are raised by Lewis's curious relationship with Stowe. They include race, pride in authorship, and money. Examining these issues is important in order to provide a clearer understanding of how the relationship influenced Lewis's life.

Was race a factor in the way Stowe treated Lewis? There is no direct indication in the literature that Clarke was intentionally treated poorly by Stowe because of his race. When Lewis spoke of her contributions to blacks in particular and the nation as a whole, he describes her with the highest praise. When informed of her death, he said, "I am sorry to hear that this good woman has been called into the great beyond. In the death of Mrs. Stowe the country loses one of the greatest emancipators the world has ever known, and I believe that had it not been for her story *Uncle Tom's Cabin* we would be all slaves today.[114] That book threw fierce light on the institution of slavery under which it was compelled to perish. We were individually trying to show the people in the North just what slavery was, but we [including Frederick Douglass] were unable to reach the masses properly, and it remained for Mrs. Stowe to do this . . . Lewis Tappan, Dr. William Goodell, William Lloyd Garrison, Wendell Phillips and Cassius Clay had written and spoken volumes against slavery, but the Yankee school mistress struck a moral chord greater than the others were able to do and the result was that the great human heart of the nation was touched and slavery was ultimately abolished."[115]

In his praise of her, Lewis is also giving credit to himself. In the same interview he said that he "read her story as it appeared in the *National Era* and I recognized the facts I had told her six years before at Mrs. Safford's."[116] Concerning *Uncle Tom's Cabin*, he said that it was denounced in the severest terms, especially in the South; however, "such a work was needed and it greatly helped the cause. The only fault I had with it was that it did not tell in language strong enough the woes of the slaves who were branded with hot irons, starved, whipped, trampled upon and otherwise cruelly treated."[117]

In later years, Stowe was accused of being racist by such well-known figures as civil rights activist Malcolm X, author James Baldwin, intellectual James Weldon Johnson, and black intellectuals generally, because they saw the subservient way many of the black characters were depicted in the novel. Influenced by such notables, many detractors either failed to recall or ignored the fact that the title character, Uncle Tom, painted a different, more nuanced picture of the man. Tom heroically preferred to be beaten to death rather than reveal the whereabouts of two women slaves to the evil master Simon Legree. The scene contrasted the evil of Legree with the Christian like Tom, which resulted in the reader having more empathy for the slave. In today's world, Tom's actions would be defined as a nonviolent civil disobedience tactic of the kind promoted by Dr. Martin Luther King and his followers during the Civil Rights Movement of the 1950s and 1960s. King and demonstrators against apartheid in the South allowed themselves to be beaten by police without defending themselves. Critics of the approach said that it was against human nature to be beaten without responding in kind. Not reacting in the same manner demonstrated, from their perspective, weakness of character. During the civil rights rebellions, television news and photographs in the print media left indelible imprints of the evil police atrocities for the world to see. Those scenes had the desired outcome. Popular support against discriminatory laws increased with the ultimate result being the passage of the Civil Rights Act of 1964. During the 1960s, watching billy-club wielding Sheriff Bull Connor of Birmingham, Alabama, beating black teenage Freedom Riders on television was similar to Stowe describing slave master Simon Legree whipping a defenseless Uncle Tom to death. To endure such treatment for the greater good is a strength, not a weakness. The images of the evils of discrimination based upon race were seared into the hearts and minds of Americans in both situations and the desired empathy for the movements resulted. That was the intended outcome perceived by King as well as Stowe and her mentors.

The desire by some to paint Stowe as a racist should not be a relevant issue of discussion if one assumes that *Uncle Tom's Cabin* was written as a political/propaganda treatise with the intent of convincing the North that slavery needed to be abolished. Within that context the mission was successful.

Frederick Douglass also gave Stowe great praise for her writing of *Uncle Tom's Cabin*: "In the midst of the passage of the Fugitive Slave Act, came the book known as *Uncle Tom's Cabin*, a work of marvelous depth and power. Nothing could have better suited the morale and humane requirements of the hour. Its effect was amazing, instantaneous and universal. No book on the subject of slavery had so generally and favorably touched the American heart. It combined all the power and pathos of preceding publications of the kind."[118] Nevertheless, Stowe and Douglass had their differences concerning the direction of the abolitionist movement.

There was an incident that challenged the veracity and integrity of either Douglass or Stowe, depending upon whom one would choose to believe. According to Douglass, soon after the publication of her novel, Harriet Beecher Stowe contacted him and invited him to her home in Andover, Massachusetts (similar to the Clarke invitation). Douglass was delighted to have the opportunity to meet the great author for the first time. The object of Stowe's meeting was to discuss what could be done to assist free colored people of the country. Stowe said she wanted a monument to *Uncle Tom's Cabin*, something that would show that it produced more than a transient influence. Douglass responded by pointing out that the need for money was the root of all evil to colored people and that having trade schools where blacks could learn skills leading to employment would be the best direction she could go. Mrs. Stowe asked Douglass to put his thoughts in writing and send her a letter. He complied with her wishes. It is important to note that Stowe had promised Douglass that she would seriously consider his request if he ceased making public attacks against William Lloyd Garrison concerning their differences.

Douglass sent a long letter to Stowe dated March 8, 1853, proposing the establishment of a national trade college that would prepare students to go directly from the school to relevant jobs. Douglass, in July 1853, presented the outline of his letter to a large assemblage of blacks at a convention in Rochester, New York. The attendees were delighted with Douglass's remarks, which also received widespread attention throughout the United States and abroad. In the meantime, while Stowe was in Europe, she was attacked vigorously by the press for receiving money for her own private use as a result of the sales of *Uncle Tom's Cabin*. Stowe's brother Henry Ward Beecher felt that the accusations against Harriet had to be addressed. He then asked Douglass to relay to the detractors what Stowe intended to do with the money. Douglass placated the accusers and assured them that the money was to be used for the establishment of an industrial school for colored youth. The information was circulated in the media, and the attacks ceased. After Harriet returned to the United States, Douglass was enraged to learn that Stowe had changed her position concerning the industrial school. Embarrassed, Douglass was never given any reason by Stowe for the change of mind."[119]

According to Stowe biographer Joan Hedrick, the meeting of Douglass with Mrs. Stowe was initiated by Douglass, not Stowe. Hedrick pointed out that from Stowe's father's experience from Lane Seminary, she was not "sanguine" about the benefits of manual labor schools. According to Stowe, Douglass persisted using his antislavery paper [*North Star*] to keep his scheme alive. Others began to wonder why Stowe was not backing Douglass's proposal in view of all the money she had reaped from *Uncle Tom's Cabin*. The indignant Stowe coldly and insensitively burst out to abolitionist Wendell Phillips, "Of all the vague unbased [*sic*] fabrics of vision, this floating idea of a colored industrial school [by Douglass] is the most elusive. If *they* want one why don't *they* have one—many men among the colored people are richer than I am—better able to help such an object. Will *they* ever learn to walk?"[120]

The Frederick Douglass conflict questions again Stowe's veracity. The stories of Douglass and Stowe are so far apart, the conflict is difficult to dismiss as a miscommunication. An astute public figure like Douglass making such an important announcement to the public without receiving assurances from Mrs. Stowe is hard to fathom.

Douglass's account of Henry Beecher asking him to publicly defend Stowe, knowing that Stowe had no intention of backing up her commitment for the industrial school, was especially heinous. Clearly, Douglass was used and left twisting in the wind by Stowe and her brother. Ever the statesman, Douglass wrote of the incident, "Her change in purpose was a great disappointment, and placed me in an awkward position before colored people of this country, as well as to friends abroad, to whom I had given assurances that the money would be appropriated in the manner I have described."[121]

Stowe's pattern of disrespect was also reflected in an incident that took place before her trip to Europe. 'She received a letter on behalf of Harriet Jacobs, a former slave. Jacobs was living in New York City as a maid in the home of Nathaniel and Cornelia Willis, where Jacobs was also raising the Willis's children. The letter asked for literary advice from Stowe regarding a story Jacobs was writing about her life as a slave. The circumstances surrounding her bondage were very dramatic. She had vivid testimony that if slavery was terrible for men, it was far more dramatic for women."[122] She was harassed by her master, who was determined to make her his mistress. Jacobs, on her own volition, established another relationship with another white man who was a Whig candidate for the US Congress, by whom she had two children. Jacobs hid for seven years in an attic crawl space too small for her to stand up. She managed to elude her slave master and the bonds of slavery while living in the attic. She felt that the excitement surrounding the Fugitive Slave Law of 1850 made the time right to tell her story. Although Jacobs was embarrassed about her sexual history, she asked Quaker abolitionist Amy Post to write to Stowe describing her life in detail. Jacobs realized the risk, because her employer did not know the circumstances that led to the birth of her children. Stowe's response shocked Jacobs. She sent Post's letter directly to Jacob's employer, inquiring whether the profound story was true, and if so whether she might use it in the book she was preparing, *The Key to Uncle Tom's Cabin.*

Both Harriet Jacobs and her employer were stunned by Stowe's revelation of Jacobs's history. Jacobs wrote to Amy Post that "my employer knew that it embarrassed me at first but we both thought it was wrong of Mrs. Stowe to have sent the letter. She might have written to enquire."[123] When Stowe realized that Jacobs wanted to write her own story and wanted to supply her with "some facts for her book" but not Stowe's narrative, Stowe did not answer any of the four subsequent letters that she sent.

Joan Hedrick cogently observed that Stowe's behavior was "an extreme example of insensitivity bred by class and skin privilege was probably exacerbated by her sense of literary 'ownership' of the tale of the fugitive slave. Wedded to the notion that she 'spoke for the oppressed, who cannot speak for themselves,' she tried in this instance to appropriate the story of a former slave."[124] Was this an isolated instance to "appropriate a story of a former slave"? The Lewis Clarke experience shows clear similarities. Hedrick's observation regarding the mind-set of Stowe gives credence to Lewis Clarke's contention for years, that his slave narrative and conversations with Stowe constituted a framework for *Uncle Tom's Cabin*. Hedrick also provides an insightful perspective on Stowe's mind-set vis-à-vis blacks for her insensitive and patronizing treatment of Douglass, Jacobs, and Clarke.

Stowe's general insensitivity toward blacks was demonstrated in what became known as the penny offering incident. Unprecedented income was derived from sales of *Uncle Tom's Cabin* in Great Britain. A penny offering from each reader was contributed to the author from throughout the British Isles because Stowe did not receive royalties from the sale of her book in England. The offering allowed her to take home beyond $20,000. This led a way to observe that such an amount of money would allow the well-known abolitionist William Lloyd Garrison to make a living and Stowe a fortune out of the cause of colored people.[125] Most of the contributors gave their pennies with the desire for Stowe to do something for the cause of the slave. Including the $20,000 Stowe received from the penny offering, she accumulated over $60,000 over an eighteen-month period from the proceeds of the book. Sensing trouble when she arrived back in the United States with such a large amount of money, her husband, Calvin, warned that many people would be clawing for money. From the theme of her novel, one would assume that Stowe would be bound by conscience and public opinion to use a significant portion of her earnings to promote the antislavery theme of her novel.

The monetary needs of Stowe's large family influenced how she managed her windfall. As an example, her sister Catherine provided assistance in the writing of the novel and also ran her household while she was gone. Harriet rightly felt obligated to be generous to her. Also brother Charles was on Harriet's payroll as her secretary and travel agent while in Europe. Her brother James was given $2,000 and her children, particularly her teenage twins, needed large sums for their education. Clearly the funds were melting away. Stowe talked about a "permanent memorial to the colored race." However, no memorial came from the funds accumulated from the $20,000 penny offering although that was the expectation from donors. The disposition of the money became a mystery. Stowe likely mixed the offerings within her personal accounts. Pressured by public criticism for not using the money for the cause, it led her to give $6,000 in 1856 for the purchase of books, periodicals, and the "promotion of education among colored people." With no specifics, there was no further mention of support for a permanent memorial to blacks along the lines nor of the scale she had discussed with Frederick Douglass. Of the $60,000 accumulated during the time of her tour of Europe, the overwhelming portion of the fortune was utilized for her personal well-being.[126]

Stowe's actions toward blacks were generally consistent with what George Frederickson called romantic racialism, a blend of humanitarian and paternalistic attitudes toward blacks. The theory begins with the assumption that blacks were inferior to whites socially and intellectually but emphasized their lightheartedness and willingness to serve as natural Christians, whose attributes allowed them to attain a level of Christianity unavailable to the naturally aggressive Caucasians. This view had great appeal in the North, as reflected by the popularity of *Uncle Tom's Cabin*. The philosophy provided an implicit excuse for Anglo-Saxon aggressiveness, including mistreatment of other races. If such a tendency were "in the blood," it would inevitably find outlets, regardless of how morally objectionable the consequences would be. The theory implicitly deprived blacks of the inherent ability to compete on equal terms with the aggressive Anglo-Saxons. An early formulator of this ideology was Alexander Kinmont, who lectured in Cincinnati from 1837 to 1838 at the same time Stowe was living there. She likely heard him lecture or read his material. Fredrickson observed, "Whatever the circumstances of her first encounter with Kilmont's ideas and whatever influence they may have had at the time, their presence in *Uncle Tom's Cabin* seems indisputable."[127] The romantic racialism theory was not only reflected in Stowe's writing but was clearly practiced in her personal dealings with blacks as the aforementioned examples describe.

It was an "unabashed fact that she wrote for money."[128] Clarke observed in the early 1840s that she did not display much passion or knowledge of the slavery issue. He claimed that it was not until Lewis Tappan approached her to write a series of articles in the *National Era* about slavery, which led to the publication of *Uncle Tom's Cabin*, that she saw the opportunity to take advantage of the notes Clarke had dictated to her. The opportunity was money. Tappan knew of her dire financial situation. The implication was that her "fervor" for the slavery issue began at that point.

Even Stowe acknowledged that the need for money was a primary factor behind her writing *Uncle Tom's Cabin*: "On looking back to the time when *Uncle Tom's Cabin* came forth, I see myself then a woman with no particular capital of reputation, driven to write then as now by the necessity of making some income for family expenses. In this mood, with my mind burning with the wrongs of slavery, I undertook to write some loose sketches of slave life in the *National Era*, and out of the attempt grew *Uncle Tom's Cabin*."[129]

Clarke was spot on in detecting in the early 1840s the lack of passion demonstrated by Stowe concerning the slave issue. It is not unusual for a writer to rationalize excitement about a topic or a cause when there is the possibility of a significant financial return. The rationalization can become a strong belief. This very well could have been the circumstance regarding Stowe. The question is whether her avariciousness was such that she did not want to give anyone, including Clarke, due credit for any aspect of her story in order not to share royalties from the sale of the book. Her actions over a period of years support this contention.

Although race was a factor in the crude way Harriet Beecher Stowe treated Lewis Clarke, among others, it should not be regarded as the primary reason behind their ill treatment by Stowe. She responded indignantly if anyone implied that she was not committed to bettering the circumstances of blacks in America. Her commitment against slavery could not be besmirched. The driving force throughout her entire adult life was the accumulation of wealth to ensure the financial stability of her family. In the process, she and family members ruffled feathers without regard to race or color.

As late as 1870, eighteen years after the publication of *Uncle Tom's Cabin*, Stowe had no compunctions about declaring that she wrote *Uncle Tom's Cabin* because she was "driven then as now by the necessity of making some income for family expenses." Her literary focus on the wrongs of slavery was the vehicle for that necessity. The conflicts she had with blacks, i.e., Clarke, Douglass, and Jacobs, were fundamentally around the issue of money. Whether the matter was the building of a vocational school, protection of her estate from claims of royalty rights, fear of revelations regarding appropriating stories of slaves without their knowledge or approval—it was all related to maintaining and accumulating wealth. She had no reservations about such acts because doubters would only have to reflect upon what she had done for blacks by writing the book that helped free them. Her financial motivations do not diminish the importance of *Uncle Tom's Cabin* in helping to turn the nation against slavery.

Harriet Beecher Stowe was a product of the Victorian era. As Melville aptly observed, "The great figures of history are parts of the times, they themselves are the times and possess a corresponding coloring." She had a paternalistic view of what she considered best for slaves and Lewis in particular. Because of her social and intellectual "superiority," she felt it was her duty to protect the weak even though in doing so she would violate basic precepts of morality. The relationship Stowe had with Lewis was rife with examples of that attitude. Surprisingly, arch conservative, former British Prime Minister Margaret Thatcher was reported as saying that she would be pleased to restore all the Victorian virtues with the exception of hypocrisy. Clearly, Stowe believed her hypocritical relationship with Lewis was, from her perception, for the greater good of Clarke and blacks in general.

Chapter 4

A Leading Spokesman For
The Abolitionist Cause

For over fifteen years, while living in Cambridge, Clarke delivered over five hundred antislavery speeches in the Northeast and Canada before assemblies numbered in the thousands. Early on, when asked to speak, he tended to be more engaging in small groups and came across as more stiff when addressing large audiences. His abolitionist advisors wanted him to be "displayed" before large gatherings because of his riveting experiences as a slave. Because of Lewis's lack of education, his initial forays into the world of public speaking were not auspicious.

When the uneducated Clarke addressed a large antislavery audience in Brooklyn in 1842, Lydia M. Child observed, "His obvious want of education was one guarantee of the truth of his story, and the uncouth awkwardness of his language had a sort of charm, like the circuitous expression, and stammering utterance, of a foreign tongue, striving to speak our most familiar phrases. His mind was evidently full of ideas, which he was eager to express; but the medium was wanting. 'I've got it here,' he said, laying his hand on his heart; but I don't know how to get it out.' However, in his imperfect way, I believe he conveyed much information to many minds; and that few who heard him went away without being impressed by the conviction that he was sincerely truthful, and testified of things which he did know."[130]

After being educated for years with the Saffords in Cambridge, his speeches improved considerably. He became a witty, engaging, and polished speaker, as coverage from newspaper articles and convention proceedings over the years attest. A letter published in the *National Anti-Slavery Standard* indicated that less than a year after escaping from slavery, some who attended Clarke's speeches questioned his authenticity. The *Standard* said, "Some time ago, we published an account of the fugitive slave, [Lewis Clarke] under the head of 'Leaves from a Slave's Journal of Life.' He has since been lecturing in various parts of the country. In [the State of] Maine he was charged with being an impostor; probably because he is so white. In consequences of this, the editor of the *Standard* wrote to the Hon. J. R. Giddings, a well-known abolitionist, and a member of the U. S. House of Representatives from the State of Ohio, who replied as follows:

Washington City, Jan. 3, 1843.

My Dear Sir: - Your favor of the 27th reached me by this evening's mail. I am acquainted with Lewis Clark. A brother is Milton Clark was arrested last fall, by some slave hunters, in the vicinity in which I reside. He was released by habeas corpus. I understood they were anxious to get hold of Lewis, who was near his brother at the time of his arrest, but avoided the men-hunters. A night or two subsequently, Lewis Clark, in the company of his brother, and some other friends, came to consult with me professionally. This was the first time I ever saw him, although he had been long acquainted at Oberlin [Ohio] and the gentleman who recommended him to me as a shrewd man, and a fugitive from slavery. The slave-hunters related the history of those brothers very nearly as they did themselves. I have no doubt, the story is *substantially* true." [131]

Austin Willey, a leading abolitionist in Maine, attended the Eighth Annual Meeting of the Maine Anti-Slavery Society in Hallowell on January 18 and 19, 1843, and witnessed a featured speech delivered by Lewis: "Lewis Clarke, a fugitive slave, was present and greatly increased the interest of the meeting. He was a remarkable young man for ability, good sense, social qualities and public speaking. Few could reach the hearts of an audience like him, and he did the cause of his people great service." Willey added that Clarke "stayed in the state several weeks lecturing and attending meetings with me in Oxford, Franklin, Somerset, Cumberland and Lincoln . . . Mr. Clarke's form was manly, his countenance open and intelligent, and his mental powers wonderful in his condition . . . To look upon him as a slave was amazing. He was a fugitive from Kentucky, and his personal history horrible, but so honestly stated that no one could doubt its perfect truth." Willey and Clarke remained lifetime friends.[132]

Henry Bibb, the famous fugitive slave, orator, and publisher of the Canadian antislavery publication, *Voice of the Fugitive,* observed in 1847 after a recent visit to Boston, "I had the pleasure. . . of taking by the hand, Mr. [Lewis] Clark of Boston. He is a self-emancipated slave and is as white as most white people; he is also the first fugitive in this country that opened his mouth to expose the evils of American Slavery in public. I hope he may be prevailed upon to spend some time in Michigan before he returns to the East. He is an intelligent and interesting speaker, has traveled all over New England, and is much esteemed by his fellow citizens."[133]

Bibb's observation is enlightening. Most historians have intimated that Frederick Douglass was the first fugitive slave to lecture about the evils of slavery in the United States. Clearly that was not the case. Even though Douglass had been giving antislavery speeches in the United States since 1842, as was Clarke, Douglass wanted to make sure his audiences did not know that he was a *fugitive* slave. In a speech on May 18, 1846, in London, Douglass pointed out that after delivering antislavery speeches for four years, "My manner was such as to create a suspicion that I was not a runaway slave, but some educated free negro, whom abolitionists had sent forth to attract attention to what was called a faltering cause. They said, 'he appears to have no fear of white people. How can he ever have been in bondage?' But one strong reason for this doubt was the fact that I never made known to the people to whom I spoke where I came from. . . but it became necessary to set myself right before the public in the United States, and to reveal the whole facts of my case. I did not feel to do so till last spring, when I was solicited to it by a number of anti-slavery friends, who assured me that it would be safe to do so [i.e., William Lloyd Garrison and Wendell Phillips]. I then published a narrative of my experience in slavery, in which I detailed the cruelties of it as I had myself felt them."[134]

Douglass went on an extensive speaking tour in Great Britain immediately after his 1845 *Narrative* was published. His master, Hugh Auld of Maryland, became incensed by how his family was depicted by Douglass in his book and pledged to "place him in the cotton fields of the South" if he ever returned to the United States. Douglass did not return to the United States until 1846, after two British abolitionists, Anna and Ellen Richardson, bought Douglass from Auld. Auld signed the manumission papers that made Douglass a free man.[135] Lewis Clarke, on the other hand, made it clear during his lectures that he was a fugitive slave with slave catchers from Kentucky in hot pursuit. He had no intention of purchasing his freedom from his slave master. To do so would have given credence to the so-called right of one man owning another. Clarke was also known to carry pistols with him for protection.

The story of Lewis Clarke and his efforts to free himself and his brothers from slavery spread throughout the Northeast. Clarke and his brother Milton were the pioneers among escaped slaves in platform lecturing, but they may not have met the goals of abolitionist leaders were seeking as clearly as Frederick Douglass, who came along later.

Lewis's improved speaking and debating skills were in full display when Clarke was also billed as the first slave to ever stand up in a public assembly to argue the question of slavery with a slave owner from the South. He was invited by Lewis Tappan to speak at the great Boston Convention of the Northern and Eastern Abolitionists in 1847. The convention was held at the Tremont Temple, crowded by an audience of thousands. Tappan presided over the proceedings. Clarke occupied a seat in the gallery at the side of the platform. Lewis's address about his experiences as a slave was presented to the assembly for adoption. W. W. Bryan of Lexington, Kentucky, objected to the motion. Asked why he objected, Bryan replied, "Because the address isn't true." He was then called to the stand to state his case and entered into a long argument in favor of slavery.

At the end of his argument, there was a great outcry from the audience for "Clarke! Clarke!" His four years of involvement in antislavery crusade in New England had made him familiar to anti-slavery audiences. "The call was so tumultuous that it could not be disregarded, and Clarke took the stand."

As he approached the podium, a gentleman in the audience inquired if a question was in order.

Mr. Tappan replied that "questions or statements bearing on the points were in order."

The questioner then asked if the president claimed that the gentleman about to speak was a fugitive slave from Kentucky.

Mr. Tappan replied that there was no doubt about it.

The questioner said he had been informed that the gentleman who had just spoken was a slaveholder in Kentucky, and wanted to know if that was correct.

Mr. Tappan said it was undoubtedly so.

"Then," continued the questioner, "will you please to tell me, a Jersey man who is ignorant on these topics, how it happens that the slaveholder is darker in complexion than the fugitive slave?"

Mr. Tappan replied to the Jersey man that he had often heard Mr. Clarke explain this phenomenon, and if he chose, he could explain now.

Lewis declined to do so, saying that "no one is responsible for his complexion, but as parentage has much to do with it, Mr. Bryan might explain." Lewis went on to say that it was for the slaveholder, not the slave, to answer this.

The ripples of laughter caused by this episode having passed away, Lewis stepped forward to reply to Mr. Bryan. For a moment he could not think of what to say, but when he opened his mouth to speak he became inspired and his tongue could not keep up with his thoughts. In his years of public speaking he had never found the exact words he wanted come so freely to his mind as on that occasion. He was extremely pleased with the positive reaction from the audience.

Mr. Bryan attempted a rejoinder to Clarke's remarks, but he accurately sensed that the audience did not support him. In the course of his reply, he alluded to Clarke as "my friend, the gentleman from Kentucky."

Clarke suggested that while it would be safe to speak of a slave as a gentleman in Boston, Mr. Bryan probably knew as well as anyone that such a remark in Kentucky would bring trouble upon him.

The *Boston Globe* reported the next day, "At the Tremont Convention, made up of men of prominence, character and talent; the slaveholder and the fugitive were left to fight it out alone." All who were present believed that there was no man who could appropriately wrestle with the champion of the patriarchal institution as the fugitive slave who had tested all its benefits. For the "prudent" newspapers of Boston at the time, it was unpopular to say a good word about antislavery men; however, the next morning the newspapers declared that of the two gentlemen of Kentucky, the fugitive slave was easily the victor in the contest.[136]

Another notable in the abolitionist movement to take notice of Lewis was Gerrit Smith, an upstate New York philanthropist. In a letter to Frederick Douglass, he made specific reference to escaped slaves Lewis Clarke and two of his brothers, Milton and Cyrus, regarding the deeding of land to them:[137]

Peterboro, Dec. 8, 1847

FREDERICK DOUGLASS-My Dear Sir—I welcome you to the State of New York. In this your new home [Douglass had just moved to Buffalo] may you and yours, and your labors of love for your suppressed race be all greatly blessed of God.

Above is my draft for five dollars to pay for two years' subscription to your forth coming paper [*North Star*]. Comfortably to my purpose of giving to 3000 colored inhabitants of this State the principal share of my lands, which are fit for farming. I made out 2000 deeds last year. I am now busy, with my clerks, in making out the remaining 1000. Inasmuch as you and Mr. Nell [William C. Nell, Douglass' assistant editor] have become inhabitants of the State, I feel liberty to convey a parcel of land to each of you. Herewith are the deeds. I wish the land was in less rigorous clime, but it is smooth and arable, and not wanting of fertility. Forty acres—that is, a quarter of the same lot of which I have conveyed a quarter each to yourself and Mr. Nell I have given to Mr. C. L. Redmond. The remaining quarter will probably be conveyed to Mr. W. W. Brown, who has also become an inhabitant of the State. One of the contiguous lots I have divided amongst four slaves, viz:

Henry Bibb, and the three brothers, Lewis, Milton, and
Cyrus Clark [*sic*].

With great regard,

Your friend and brother

Gerrit Smith

Lewis is identified in Smith's deed as "formerly a slave in Kentucky."
He had "frequently been in the family" of Smith and was "an inhabitant
of Peterboro." There is no evidence that the Clarke brothers settled in
Essex County, New York, where the property was located. However,
other fugitive slaves settled in the area. Smith gave to blacks and other
settlers hundreds of farms, 40 to 150 acres each. Gerrit Smith distributed
at least six thousand acres of land in the Adirondack Mountains to
free blacks and fugitive slaves and other poor blacks in St. Lawrence,
Clinton, Jefferson, Lewis, Hamilton, and Essex Counties in New York
in mid-1800. By the late 1800s the total land value was over one million
dollars. Over time the land was taken over by the state of New York
because of nonpayment of taxes. This oversight was the result of neglect
by either the Smith heirs or the descendants of the blacks who owned
the deeds. In a 1904 New York State court case, the heirs of one of
the blacks who were given hundreds of grants by Smith challenged
the takeover of the land by the state of New York, to no avail. Edwin
Cotter, the superintendent of the John Brown Farm for over thirty years,
contended that "Gerrit Smith had opened up over 100,000 acres of wild
land in New York State, much of it untamed Adirondack wilderness, for
the express purpose of small farms cultivation by Negroes."[138]

Frederick Douglass and Clarke connected in a significant way in
August 8, 1848, during the historic Free-Soil Party Convention held
in Buffalo, New York. Douglass said that it was his privilege "to attend
and participate in the famous Free Soil Convention in August. The
conviction became general that the time had come for a new organization
which should embrace all who were in any manner opposed to slavery
and the slave power and this Free-Soil convention was the result of that
conviction." He went on to say that he was not the only colored man in
attendance and mentioned Samuel R. Ward, the acclaimed Henry Bibb,

Charles Lennox, and Henry Garnet, as well as Lewis Clarke. All were active leaders in the abolitionist effort. Douglass also pointed out that "Lewis Clarke, the fugitive, was called on, and addressed the meeting for an hour, showing up slave power with force and ability." The Free Soil third party rolled up enough votes in the presidential election of 1848 to enable the Whig candidate General Zachary Taylor to win the election even though the Free Soil candidate Martin Van Buren did not carry one state. Senator Lewis Cass of Michigan was the Democrats' candidate.[139]

Lewis left Cambridge in 1849, moving to Busti, Chautauqua County, in western New York State. Milton, who remained in Cambridge, initially worked as a caterer and waiter and raised a family. In 1870, Milton succeeded his patron Aaron Safford, Stowe's brother-in-law, on the Common Council [city council] of the town, becoming its first African American elected to public office. In 1872 he resigned to become a messenger at the US Sub-Treasury in Boston. He was employed there for thirty years until his death in 1902 at the age of eighty-two.[140]

Why Lewis decided to move to Busti was the result of several factors. Lewis and Milton were undoubtedly among the first slaves to travel vast portions of the country lecturing about their experiences. They were certainly successful in that regard; however, they did not accomplish as much for the abolitionist movement as did Frederick Douglass who came along later. Aside from Douglass's superlative speaking and writing skills, color was a major drawback of Lewis and his brother. They were so white in appearance that they were looked upon with suspicion by those who were not acquainted with the facts regarding their bloodline and history.[141] Most of their white audiences generalized that slaves were black in complexion and refused to recognize the facts regarding miscegenation on the Southern plantations. Miscegenation resulted in the original black slaves becoming all gradations of color from the darkest black to the fairest white. Douglass, who was darker in complexion than either of the Clarke brothers, was hailed as the very lecturer white abolitionists were seeking. There was no reason in the eyes of the audiences to question Douglass's authenticity as a slave.[142] Although this circumstance did not dampen Lewis's fervor to abolish slavery, he may have decided to cut back from speaking at large gatherings and take on more grassroots activities on behalf of enslaved blacks. The Underground Railroad community in Busti, New York, certainly fulfilled that desire.

The impending Fugitive Slave Act of 1850, which allowed slave owners to capture escaped slaves anywhere in the United States, must have weighed upon Lewis, as the better known of the two brothers who escaped to the North. Lewis likely regarded the back woods of southwestern New York State as a safer locale than the bustling Boston area. Frederick Douglass, who had purchased his freedom in 1846, was not threatened by capture as was Lewis. Another compelling reason for Clarke moving to Busti was a love interest.

During his travels as a speaker, he often came to the tangent regions of Chautauqua County, New York, and Warren County, Pennsylvania. It was during those visits he met Catherine Storum, a beautiful mulatto from Busti, and eventually married her on June 12, 1849, by Reverend L. P. Judson. [143] In February 1850, Lewis purchased a neighboring farm from his father-in-law, abolitionist William Storum, a mulatto free slave originally from Connecticut. Clarke and his wife lived together for less than a year before she died of an undetermined illness in late 1850, leaving no children. After waiting thirty-five years to marry, the death of Catherine was clearly a devastating blow. His years as a successful leader in the abolitionist movement could not provide solace for this deep personal tragedy. After the death of Catherine, Clarke maintained close contact with his father-in-law through the late 1850s; however, Clarke would leave the Busti area for long periods of time for speaking engagements or traveling back and forth to Canada making arrangements for fugitive slaves. After the death of Catherine, the September 2, 1850 census for Busti, Chautauqua, County, New York, reflects that Lewis, then thirty-five, lived on the same tract of land as William Storum, his father-in-law, sixty-two, and his mother-in-law, Sally Storum, sixty. Clarke's portion of the tract was valued at $1,000, and Storum's was recorded as $2,000. Of the nine residents living on the tract, all were listed as mulattoes. The relationship with Mr. Storum soured in 1853 because of a dispute "mainly as to compensation for Clarke's services, but including value and ownership of the property. (The search of the abstract of title . . . leaves no doubt as to the ownership of the farm. Perhaps otherwise as to personal property.)"[144] Clarke sold the farm in 1853 but continued to have a presence in the Busti area through the 1850s.

While on the farm Clarke said he "raised seeds and afterwards brings them to Canada to distribute among the fugitive slaves who had settled there. . . . I helped the fugitives all I could and went South frequently to get for them their freedom."[145] As a conductor of the Underground Railroad, Lewis assisted slaves entering Ontario, Canada, by way of Chautauqua County, New York, and Warren County, Pennsylvania, on Lake Erie. Fundamentally, Lewis's role as the stationmaster was to lead the community effort for fugitive slaves entering New York from the South, with money, food, and a place to sleep before they moved on to Canada as well as other places in the North. While in Busti he was described by leading residents as "the most picturesque and interesting member of the Busti's colored colony in the 1850s." He became known as one of the greatest abolitionists of the day and was recognized as such in that he visited all sections of the North speaking for the antislavery cause. His lectures were not only well attended but served to keep the flames of the abolitionists burning. His neighbors saw him as ambitious and hardworking, a "man of great native ability and an effective speaker."[146]

Because of his leadership and notoriety, Lewis was selected as the president of the Warren County, Pennsylvania (three miles across the state line from Busti) Radical Abolitionists, who favored immediate emancipation of the slaves. Lewis also became well-connected with all the leading Underground Railroad leaders in the area of the Pennsylvania and New York border. The most prominent of the leaders was Jermain W. Loguen, an African Methodist Episcopal Pastor, who became well-known as the Underground Railroad King of the State of New York.

As a result of the Fugitive Slave Law of 1850, the northern states were no longer safe havens for fugitive slaves. Lewis became particularly aware of this reality when slave catchers swooped into Busti looking for him in the early 1851. The chilling episode was described in a letter dated October 1851 by a Mrs. Hunter to her husband in Charleston, South Carolina, when she was visiting her parents in Busti. In summary, Mrs. Hunter recalled the following:

> In February of 1851 seven fugitive slaves came to Busti on their way to Canada. They were seeking work and were soon hired by Mrs. Hunter's parents. Two of them decided to go back to South Carolina and bring their

wives back to Busti. One of the slaves was captured by bounty hunters and forced to reveal the whereabouts of the others. The slave catchers were able to secure warrants for arrests of the remaining slaves from a judge in Buffalo, New York.

A total of twelve slave catchers, some of whom were disguised as women, arrived in Busti and began searching for the fugitives in the homes and farms within the vicinity of the town. They arrived at the Storum farm where Mr. Storum and the fugitive slave, Harrison Williams were milking cows. Lewis Clarke was standing at the door of the Storum home where he was residing. A carriage drove up to the property and one of the slave catchers got out and asked if Lewis Clarke was home. Clarke answered that he was in the vicinity, and then quickly slammed the door shut and locked it. The slave catcher then pushed the door hard and broke the lock. Clarke ran to his room, buckled on his loaded pistols and went out the back door seeking the intruders.

In the meantime, several of the slave catchers went to the milk barn, pushed Mr. Storum aside, put chains on Harrison, forced him into the carriage and drove off. As soon as Lewis saw what was going on with Harrison he jumped on his horse in hot pursuit of the kidnappers. By the time Lewis got to Jamestown, New York, where Harrison was temporarily incarcerated, a total of more than 30 residents of Busti were after the kidnappers.

Clarke, along with an attorney attempted to get a writ of habeas corpus from a Judge Hazeltine, in Jamestown in an attempt to have Harrison released, but it was of no use since the slave catchers had the papers proving that Harrison was the property of his slave master. The Fugitive Slave Act of 1850 was in full effect. There was no safe haven for a fugitive slave anywhere in the United States.

Clarke offered $100 to purchase Harrison, if agreed upon by Harrison's master. The offer was not accepted. Mrs. Hunter observed that Clarke would not be taken without bloodshed, "He goes armed with two pistols a Bowie Knife and a lead mallet." She concluded her letter by observing "The slaveholders have left their abettors, as spies all over town, so that if fugitives should be seen, they may know it immediately and come back and grab again. *But they are all gone, except Lewis Clarke, and he will be on the lookout, and ever ready for them, and every person in the vicinity will do all that can be done to save him."*[147]

Harrison Williams was subsequently brought before Commissioner H. K. Smith of Buffalo, New York, who summarily sent Harrison back to slavery in Virginia. Twelve years later, Harrison enlisted in the Union Army.[148]

The Busti story was widely covered by the abolitionist press. Harriet Beecher Stowes's character George Harris was armed exactly as Lewis Clarke, with two pistols, a Bowie knife, and a lead mallet, when he chased the slave catchers. When George entered a small hotel in disguise and an old friend, Mr. Wilson, noticed him and advised him privately that his attempt to escape was very dangerous, George responded, "Mr. Wilson, I know all this . . . I do run a risk, but"—he threw open his overcoat, and showed two pistols and a Bowie-knife—"there! I'm ready for 'em! Down south I will never go."[149]

The passage of the Fugitive Slave Act led to frantic discussions in the north among leading black abolitionists, including Lewis. They considered three primary options: 1) moving to Canada; 2) creating a new nation(s) in the Caribbean, i.e., Haiti; or 3) remaining in the United States. Although Frederick Douglass, throughout most of his lifetime, advocated that blacks remain in this country despite their horrific circumstances, in January 1861, as war clouds gathered, he equivocated on that position. "Whatever the future may have in store for us, it seems plain that inducements offered. . . to remain here are few, feeble, and very uncertain." That statement was contrary to the response he made to Harriett Beecher Stowe in 1852 regarding her advocating the colonization of American blacks in Africa at the end of *Uncle Tom's Cabin*. "The truth is, dear madam, we are here and here we are likely to remain."[150] The brilliant black physician and abolitionist Martin Delany was consistent in his view that American blacks should leave the United States and set up a nation or colony elsewhere. He became the leading black advocate of the back-to-Africa movement.

Many other black abolitionists began to feel the same as Clarke concerning the feasibility of escaped slaves relocating to Canada. Two highly regarded fugitive slaves, Henry Bibb and Samuel R. Ward, established newspapers in Ontario, Canada, during the early 1850s and used their publications to encourage others to join them in Canada. Bibb, in August of 1851, made a call for a North American Convention for slaves to flee to Canada. He stated the following in his article:

> Dear Brethren: After a multipherity [*sic*] of correspondence with men of intelligence both in Canada and the States, on the propriety of holding a Great Northern Convention of colored freemen this fall to deliberate upon the sad condition of our people, we are led to the conclusion that the time has fully come when the combined wisdom of our best and wisest men should be concentrated on some general plan for the elevation of our race, and their future advancement.

> WE are satisfied that there is no spot in the United States where we would be safe or expedient to hold such a convention. Under the existing state of things it would greatly endanger the liberty of thousands of self-emancipated persons who gladly meet with us on such an occasion.

> On the other hand, Canada is emphatically the only land of safety on the American continent for he hunted refugees. She bids defiance to all fugitive slave laws, and protects the colored man in the enjoyment of that liberty with which he is endowed by the great Author of his existence.

We have therefore decided on the city of Toronto
Canada West, as being the most suitable place to hold
such a convention.

The article outlined nine objectives to be discussed that Fall
in Toronto. The primary one was "The immediate and everlasting
emancipation of our race from slavery and the manifestation of gratitude
of Great Britain which has nobly protected us in the enjoyment of liberty
whenever and wherever we have stepped upon her soil." Seventy-one were
asked to attend, including Lewis Clarke of Busti and brother Milton
of Cambridgeport, Massachusetts. Other well-known black leaders of
the antislavery movement invited included Dr. Martin Delaney, Rev.
Henry H. Garrett, James Grant, Samuel. R. Ward, and Rev. Josiah
Henson, depicted as Uncle Tom in Harriet Beecher Stowe's famous
novel. Interestingly, Frederick Douglass was not on the invitation list.
By the time of the convention, Douglass had purchased his freedom
from his owner in Maryland. As such he did not have to encounter the
danger of bounty hunters seeking to return him to slavery.[151]

A follow-up gathering by the Continental League of the Africo-
American Race, called the North American Convention of Colored
People, in Amherstburg, Ontario, Canada, was held on June 16 and
17, 1853. Canadian blacks dominated the meeting. The minutes of the
convention reflect that Lewis, by this time, was a resident of Sandwich,
Ontario, and served as one of the organization's vice presidents. The
president was Josiah Henson (a prototype of Uncle Tom) from Dresden,
Canada West. Several committees were established covering the areas
of emigration, agriculture, temperance, statistics, education, and
the Constitution for the Provincial League. Clarke served on three:
Emigration, Temperance, and Constitution for the Provincial League.
[152]

The report of the Emigration Committee was regarded as the
main order of business. James T. Holly, Coleman Freeman, and Lewis
Clarke constituted the committee. Their committee concluded that
slavery and oppression in the United States left black Americans with
two alternatives—revolution or emigration. While revolution was "the
most glorious" alternative, it was not practical; instead the committee
urged blacks to leave the United States. The report also recommended
that Canada or the British West Indies as "first considerations," Haiti

as a black republic, or specific sites in Central or South America as points of "secondary interest" but insisted that blacks must leave the United States. The report represents one of the few instances when black abolitionists publicly endorsed the concept of armed revolution as a possible alternative to slavery.[153,154]

It is important to note that the esteemed Dr. Martin Delaney of Pennsylvania, a convener of the first convention of this group in Toronto, did not attend the 1853 convention. He was the leader of the back-to-Africa (Liberia) American Colonization Society, which was not supported by the Amherstburg attendees. The convention also made a special resolution thanking "Mrs. Harriet Beecher Stowe for her faithful exposure of American Slavery through *Uncle Tom's Cabin,* together with her sympathy for the oppressed free colored people of the United States and asking for her support for the refugees in Canada."[155]

Documentation reflecting the transfer of slave Lewis Clarke from the estate of his grandfather Samuel Campbell to John and Elizabeth Campbell Banton. The "property" shown indicates "one Negro boy by the name of Lewis, seven years old…$225.00. (Files from Garrard County, Kentucky Court, September 6, 1823.)

Historical marker for the village of Paint Lick, Garrard County, Kentucky near the plantation of General Thomas Kennedy where Lewis Clarke was held a slave for ten years. Harriet Beecher Stowe's novel "Uncle Tom's Cabin" begins at Paint Lick.

Historical marker at the Garrard County Courthouse at the county seat Lancaster, Kentucky where Lewis Clarke was to be sold in August 1841. He fled north to Canada before the transaction could be consummated.

The Old Tavern in Unionville, Ohio where Milton Clarke was released from the custody of Kentucky slave-catchers by a local magistrate in 1842.

GREAT ANTI-SLAVERY
MEETINGS!!

LEWIS CLARK, MILTON CLARK and CYRUS
CLARK, all White Men,
Sons of a Revolutionary Soldier, and all fugitives
from southern slavery, will relate their tales of suf-
fering while in bondage, and in escaping therefrom,
in the Universalist Meeting-house, at Weymouth,
next SATURDAY and SUNDAY EVENINGS,
9th and 10th inst.
Meetings will commence at six o'clock.
Collections will be taken to aid them.
A. N. HUNT,
JOHN W. LOUD,
JOHN M. SPEAR,
Weymouth, Dec. 5th, 1843.

John A. Green, Printer, Quincy.

Advertisement of anti-slavery meeting in Weymouth, Mass.
where Lewis Clarke and his brothers Milton and Cyrus
were scheduled to tell their stories of enslavement in 1843.
(Courtesy of the Massachusetts Historical Society)

Lewis Clarke, 1845. (Courtesy of the New York Public Library)

Frederick Douglass, 1845. (Courtesy of the New York Public Library)

J. Milton Clarke, 1846. (Courtesy of the New York Public Library)

Harriet Beecher Stowe, 1852. (Courtesy of the New York Public Library)

Lewis Tappan, New York financier, a founder of the
American Anti-Slavery Society and mentor to Lewis Clarke,
1854. (Courtesy of the New York Public Library)

The Lewis Clarke family in Oberlin, Ohio, July 4 1874.
Brother Cyrus stands in the rear. Lewis's, wife Emiline, sits in
front with children on her lap. Cyrus H. Clarke, stands next
to his uncle. (Courtesy of the Oberlin College Archives)

Lewis Clarke at his spinning wheel as he appeared
during his lecture tours during the 1880's.

Lewis Clarke (The original George Harris of Uncle Tom's
Cabin) Painted from life in Oberlin, Ohio by F. H. Dart in
1885 (Courtesy of Western Reserve Historical Society)

Lewis Clarke (circa 1890)

The author is seen at Saint Paul's First AME Church the site where Lewis Clarke's funeral was held on December 19, 1897.

Cyrus H. Clark, marriage photo, to Guela Johnson, 1901, son of Lewis and Emiline Clarke and father of Virginia Clark Gayton.

Guela Johnson Clark, marriage photo, 1901,
mother of Virginia Clark Gayton.

Minnie Clarke Davis, Lewis and Emiline Clarke's
daughter and aunt of Virginia Clark Gayton, 1907.

Grand-children of Lewis and Emiline Clarke. Rear: Cyrus H. Clark Jr., Virginia Clark; front: Ruth Clark, James Clark and John Clark. (circa 1919)

John and Virginia Clark Gayton, 1967

First cousins Virginia Clark Gayton and Raymond Davis, son
of Lewis Clarke's daughter Minnie Clarke Davis, 1972.

Virginia Clark Gayton, 1988

Great-grandchildren of Lewis and Emiline Clarke and children of John and Virginia Clark Gayton. From the left: the author; Sylvia G. Wesley; Gary D. Gayton; Guela G. Johnson; John C. Gayton; Elaine G. Whitehead; Leonard M. Gayton; and Philip H. Gayton, 1993.

Carver Clark Gayton holding image of his great-grandfather
Lewis Clarke, 2004. (Courtesy of the Seattle Times)

PART II

Chapter 5

Canada Becomes Home

By 1853, Lewis had moved permanently to Sandwich, Ontario, Canada, his flight no doubt precipitated by his near capture by slave hunters in Busti. Also, sad memories of his wife's demise certainly led to a desire to start life anew in Canada. Additionally, financial conflicts with his former in-laws, the Storums, certainly made the environment in Busti more than uncomfortable for Lewis. Although living in Canada, Clarke continued his missions back to Busti and Sugargrove, Pennsylvania, to help fugitive slaves relocate to Canada. He was assisted by abolitionist organizations such as the Sugargrove Radical Abolitionist Party. His visits to the United States were not wholly on behalf of the antislavery cause. Clarke developed another love interest in Pennsylvania.

Lewis courted Clarissa Catlin of Erie County, Pennsylvania, near Busti, after the death of his wife Catherine. His relationship with the white Miss Catlin caused some consternation within her family. Evidently, Clarke being black and not formally educated were the upsetting factors. Clarissa's brother, Dr. James Catlin, was the publisher of the antislavery newspaper *True American*, in the town of Erie. He was also considered a close friend of Lewis's, at least until he started courting his sister. On February 2, 1854, Frederick Miles, a friend of the Catlins, in a letter to his niece Jane Miller Payne, stated the following:

> Sometime last week Catherine [Miller] and Clarissa
> Catlin made a visit to some friends in the state of New
> York, they took with them Lewis Clarke. I am not

prepared to say in what capacity he went. Whether as co-visitor to be ushered into a parlor with them and to be seated between them in a bees-hive settee with one around each, or whether he attended them as a menial servant of his here, and had a cold corner in some kitchen during their stay, I on this am not informed. If my recollection serves me, I did not tell you that the relatives in Erie County have heard that L. Clarke was making court to Clarissa Catlin, they were a good deal rashed up on the subject.[156]

The pressure from the relatively "liberal" community of Erie County was too much for the lovers to withstand, and they broke off their relationship. Clarissa never courted again after Lewis and died unmarried. Whether Clarissa never married out of her own volition or was considered tainted in the eyes of her family and community because of her relationship with a black man and therefore regarded "unmarriageable" is not known. The Miles letter made clear that Clarissa's relatives were embarrassed by the pairing. The negative reactions from Clarissa's relatives against Clarke in the small and close-knit Busti community did not bode well for him having a pleasant living experience in the town.

While a resident of Sandwich, Ontario, Clarke continued to be a sought-after speaker in communities throughout Northern United States. He risked his freedom as well as his life by appearing at various large gatherings in America. Frederick Douglass and Clarke crossed paths again in Chautauqua County, New York, in June of 1854. Douglass wrote in a letter to the *North Star* newspaper that he had been invited to Chautauqua County to attend a series of meetings by Reverend J. W. Loguen of Syracuse, Lewis Clarke's brother-in-law, his wife's sister's husband. The meetings were planned by Loguen, who asked Douglass to assist him in holding them. Douglass said the people in Chautauqua consisted of a good many Free Soilers, genuine abolitionists, as well as a majority of people who were ready to strike out against slavery, which was the primary subject of his meetings.

Douglass concluded his report to the *North Star* by saying after the last meeting in the area that "I never attended an out-door meeting which was as orderly and impressive as that at Sugar Grove yesterday.

The meeting was strictly a religious anti-slavery event, and left a most favorable impression for the cause. In addition to the speeches made by brother Loguen and myself, Lewis Clarke, well known as an efficient and Anti-Slavery speaker, addressed the people to marked acceptance."[157] The Sugar Grove Historical Society notes, "The Sugar Grove Anti-Slavery Convention of 1854 boasted keynote speakers Frederick Douglass, Rev. J. W. Loguen and Lewis G. Clarke, the real life George Harris of Uncle Tom's Cabin. This event helped secure Sugar Grove its place in history as one of the leading communities in the fight against slavery."

A few weeks after the successful Sugar Grove convention, Clarke was invited to deliver one of the keynote addresses at the first convention of the newly formed Republican Party on July 6, 1854, in Jackson, Michigan. Drawn by a common purpose of Whigs, Free Soilers, and Anti-Nebraska Democrats, five thousand delegates came to Jackson to protest the threat of spreading slavery. It was in Jackson where the Republican Party was organized with the adoption of a platform and the nomination of a full state ticket. Many places, especially Ripon, Wisconsin, claim the birthplace of the party, but it was at the Jackson Convention where the new party was labeled "Republican."[158] A witness's account of the proceedings gave praise to Clarke by saying that "a speech by fugitive slave Lewis Clarke, often cited as the prototype of George Harris in *Uncle Tom's Cabin,* dramatized the moment in history. Clarke, son of a Revolutionary War soldier and a Kentucky Negro girl, related how his family was sold on the auction block and how he finally managed to escape to freedom in Canada."[159] In a seventy-fifth anniversary celebration of the convention, held in Jackson in 1929, Mrs. Eleanor Gridley, who had attended the July 6, 1854, proceedings with her father, had vivid memories of the convention. She said the well-known Lewis Clarke was given a tremendous ovation when he was introduced. She also observed that "the great men on the platform talked and talked, and the colored man [Clarke] also talked and the people cheered him, and I with excitement, cheered loud and lustily and begged my father to let me speak to the hero, but my request was not granted and my disappointment was a bitter one."[160] Convention Secretary Conover's official report of the proceedings that day stated that "another pleasing incident of the meeting was a speech by Lewis Clarke, a Fugitive Slave, and the original of George Harris in *Uncle Tom's Cabin.* He was the son of a Revolutionary soldier and a Kentucky colored girl, and was then living on a farm near Sandwich, Ontario. He told how, at the death of his father, the family was sold on the auction block and how he escaped from slavery. Clarke's earnest, plain, statement had a telling effect upon the company. He was loudly and frequently applauded."[161]

Clarke's star continued to rise. He spoke at a meeting of Colored Citizens at the City Hall of Detroit on August 31, 1855. Lewis was introduced as "George Harris, of *Uncle Tom's Cabin* fame. He [Clarke] was called forth and talked at some length regarding his experiences as a slave and his involvement in the abolitionist movement. He spoke very pointedly and was listened to with much interest." The purpose of the meeting was to take action on a plan of Reverend Henry Garnett of London, Ontario, Canada, outlining how to raise funds to purchase the liberty of slaves in the Southern states.

After Clarke spoke, the following resolutions were read and unanimously adopted:

> *Resolved.* That we highly approve and cheerfully concur in the views of our brother Henry Garnett of London C. W. and bid him God speed in his great undertaking of convincing the American people that the money can be raised to purchase the liberty of slaves in the United States.
>
> *Resolved.* That we firmly believe that if every man and woman would tax himself and herself one dollar a year for the purpose of buying slaves and setting them at liberty, it would at least liberate the slaves in three states of the Union every year.
>
> *Resolved.* That we believe that the general Government [in the U. S.] has the same right to purchase slaves in Virginia, Maryland and Alabama as she has to purchase slaves found among the Seminole Indians in the Florida war.
>
> *Resolved.* That we sincerely believe in all candor that if there was less rum drank and tobacco used in this country, and the people would live more economically

in their domestic capacity the money could soon be
raised to buy every slave in the United States.

The resolutions were signed by W. C. Monroe, chairman, and J.
Lightfoot, secretary.[162]

The passage of the Kansas-Nebraska bill on May 25, 1854,
emboldened the abolitionist movement. The Kansas and Nebraska Act
called upon Congress to grant each territorial status, which questioned
the establishment of slavery within the territories. US Senator Stephen
Douglas offered a bill allowing the settlers to vote on whether they
wanted to be free or slave states. The proposed bill would make the
Missouri Compromise null and void, since that legislation stipulated
that there would be no future slavery allowed beyond the southern
border of that state.

The Kansas-Nebraska Act, along with Harriet Beecher Stowe's
Uncle Tom's Cabin, increased antislavery sentiment in the North. Direct
results were the establishment of the Republican Party and, ultimately,
the Civil War. "It is at once the worst and best bill on which Congress
ever acted," declared Senator Charles Sumner of Massachusetts. "The
worst, inasmuch as it was victory for slavery. The best, for it annuls
all past compromises with slavery, and makes all future compromises
impossible. Thus it puts freedom and slavery face to face, and bids them
to grapple. Who can doubt the result?"[163]

A guerrilla war broke out between Northern immigrants desiring
to make Kansas a free state under the popular sovereignty provision
of the Nebraska Act and the "border ruffians" who crossed the river
from Missouri to cast illicit votes to make Kansas a slave state. Heated
debates occurred in the US Senate and culminated on the Senate floor
when Congressman Preston Brooks of South Carolina delivered a savage
beating to Senator Sumner for his incendiary verbal attack on senators
Stephen Douglas of Illinois and Andrew Butler of South Carolina.
Sumner compared the old and feeble Butler to Don Quixote, "who
imagined himself to a chivalrous knight sentimentally devoted to his
beloved harlot, Slavery . . . who though ugly to others, is always lovely
to him. Riding by Butler's side, Douglas was the squire of Slavery its
very Sancho Panza, ready to do all its humiliating offices."[164]

Sumner's wife and a least one of his colleagues advised him, after seeing a draft of his speech, not to deliver it, particularly in view of its personal attacks. Two days after the speech, Butler's young cousin US Congressman Brooks approached Sumner in the Senate chambers and began beating him on the head with a heavy cane. Sumner fell unconscious and covered with blood. Returning to South Carolina, Brooks was feted throughout the South and presented with suitably inscribed canes. Braxton Bragg of Louisiana wrote, "You can only reach the sensibilities of such dogs only through their heads and a big stick." [165]

As news of the attack spread across the nation, Sumner was left with severe injuries to his brain and spinal cord, which kept him out of the Senate for three years. The North became more united than ever against slavery. Mass public meetings were convened in cities and towns throughout North to protest the beating. The caning reached into the hearts and minds of Northerners and proved to be a powerful incentive to drive independents and moderates into the newly formed Republican Party. [166]

Passage of the Kansas-Nebraska Act, followed by the caning of Senator Sumner, also precipitated frequent and more agitated protest meetings by antislavery sympathizers. At the time Lewis was president of the Radical Abolitionists of Sugar Grove, Pennsylvania, near Busti. He convened a convention, attended by blacks and whites from the surrounding area on July 26, 1856. The meeting was laced throughout with bellicose rhetoric. Lewis, as president, read the resolutions, which were adopted by the convention without opposition. The resolutions, in part, read as follows:

> Whereas, we believe that Slavery as now existing in these United States is in direct violation of the law of God, and against the inherent sense of justice implanted by the Creator in the heart of man, that it is subversive of civil and religious liberty, of the Constitution of the United States as interpreted by its Preamble ; and believing that there can be no peace to this nation while it shall be allowed an existence in our legislative enactments and whereas neither of the Political Parties proposes an abolition . . . Therefore:

1st Resolved. That in view of the position assumed by the great political . . . parties of this Nation not to interfere with slavery where it already exists . . .

2nd. Resolved. That we deeply regret the necessity forced upon us of forming a separate organization after having witnessed such exhibitions of Slavery within the last few years as we have; and we will hail with delight the auspicious day when the Republican Party, professedly Anti-Slavery, or any other, shall take the eminently just and Christian position, that man cannot be made the article of merchandise . . .

3rd. Resolved. That is laboring for the entire abolition of American Slavery, we are not only pleading the cause of the poor slave, but also for our own firesides, our own rights, the perpetuity of our own liberty, and for civil and religious liberty throughout the world.

4th. Resolved. That the treatment of Senator Sumner by Brooks, and the people of Kansas by the Border Ruffians, is but reaping what we have sowed, and *therefore we should not complain of slavery for using the only weapons—brute force, in defense of its acknowledged rights.*

5th. Resolved. That in making companions with slavery we not only suffer loss, but also acknowledge it as a system compatible with liberty and justice a position we deem wholly unsound.

6th Resolved. That we will not cease our efforts in the cause of human freedom until 'liberty is proclaimed throughout all the land to all the inhabitants thereof.

The minutes of the meeting were signed by Lewis Clarke, president, and Edgar R. Pratt, secretary, dated July 26, 1856, at Sugar Grove, Pennsylvania.[167]

The saber-rattling undercurrent of the resolutions at Sugar Grove convention suggested armed rebellion against a nation that was continually compromising on the issue of slavery. Attendees asserted that the only solution was to rid the entire nation of slavery, not just the South. The conveners hoped that the Republican Party would come forth forcefully and abolish a system that was un-Christian and contrary to the principles of the Constitution as well as the Declaration of Independence; however, they were not sanguine about that happening. Referencing the caning of Senator Sumner by Congressman Brooks, the Radical Abolitionists were very direct in the fourth resolution of the document by stating that slavery supporters had the right to defend themselves by "using the only weapons—brute force, in defense of its [their] acknowledged rights." However, the resolution clearly implied that antislavery citizens had the right to retaliate based upon the fundamental tenants of the Declaration of Independence and the US Constitution.

The nation moved closer to war between the states on March 6, 1857, with the US Supreme Court's decision on the famous *Dred Scott v. Sandford* case. Dred Scott was a slave taken by his master to Illinois to the unorganized territory north of Missouri where, according to the Missouri Compromise, slavery was forbidden. Scott came back to Missouri and sued for his freedom on the grounds that he had resided in free soil. Chief Justice Taney, speaking for the court, ruled that (1) as a Negro, Scott could not be a citizen of the United States, and therefore had no right to sue in the Federal Court; (2) as a resident of Missouri the laws of Illinois had no longer any effect on his status; and (3) as a resident of latitude 36° 30', the northern border of Missouri, he had not been emancipated because Congress had no right to deprive citizens of their property without "due process of law."[168]

At the time of the decision, Kansas was going through a referendum process to determine whether the state was to become free or open to slavery. Democrat President Buchanan asserted, on the authority of the Dred Scott decision, that "Kansas was as much a slave state as Georgia." Senator Stephen Douglas split with Buchanan on the matter, which left the Democratic Party divided and strengthened the position of the antislavery Republicans. The election of Abraham Lincoln resulted, and the clouds of war continued to gather.[169]

On March 1, 1859 the Agricultural, Mechanical, and Educational Association of Canada, West convened a meeting near Lewis Clarke's farm in East Sandwich, Ontario. The meeting was attended by many black abolitionists from the Northern states and Canada. Clarke was a founder of the association. The organization was designed to aide escaped slaves in their transition to freedom. A primary goal was to "procure suitable lands for all kinds of practical manual labor, from chopping cord wood, taking out all kinds of lumber for transportation, up to the many different kinds of workshops that may be established. Another goal was to introduce the New England style of farming and gardening—that of making a small piece of ground produce a great deal; and also to cultivate all kinds of nurseries that may be profitable. This arrangement was for the purpose of giving immediate employ to all persons just arriving from Slavery, at fair wages until they can do better."

An additional goal was to establish a "school for the benefit of slaves and others." The main hall of the school would be utilized for Christian worship with open discussion and deliberation on "all" subjects pertaining to humanitarian needs which would help eliminate the negative impacts of slavery on society. Free People, Free Speech, and Christianity was declared the motto of the school with a primary objective of it being a reformatory. The net proceeds of the enterprise would be utilized to sustain the institution. This approach toward helping newly freed slaves adjust to society through practical vocational education and positive thinking did not vary in significant ways to the educational concepts articulated years earlier by Frederick Douglass, Harriet Beecher Stowe, and after the war, by Booker T. Washington. Clarke was appointed by the trustees of the association as trustee and general traveling agent. As general traveling agent, he was "authorized to transact any pecuniary business, and to travel in the name of the Association, and to collect means for the prosecution of the group's work of Christianity and mercy—namely helping such as need help, and to be kind to the oppressed and outcast." [170]

During August of 1859, Clarke traveled to the United States for a tour de force engagement at the New England Colored Citizens' Convention at the Tremont Temple in Boston. Clarke was elected as one of the vice presidents of the meeting. The convention had been called for the purpose of "elevating the colored people of New England." Besides Clarke, keynote speakers included some of the best

known abolitionists in America, including William Lloyd Garrison
and Clarke's former brother-in-law, the Reverend J. W. Loguen of
Syracuse, the Underground Railroad King of New York. The Boston
Convention gave Lewis an excellent opportunity to promote his newly
formed Agricultural, Mechanical, and Educational Association. Before
the meeting was called to order, Clarke, for about a half hour, "kept the
audience in laughter during the whole time by his wit and the manner
in which he expressed his radical views."[171]

Within Clarke's formal remarks, he indicated that he was glad to
hear that agriculture had been laid before the meeting as the best means
of supporting one's self. He wholeheartedly approved of the approach.
Being a resident of Canada, he knew of the positive conditions there,
particularly farming and agriculture in general. He gave the example of
a small town in Canada called Buxton, which was settled in by fugitives
fifteen years earlier when the town was nothing more than dense forest.
The town grew to 850 families. Clarke emphasized that he would not
work for a man who would not work for him. He went on to say that
he wished to see the colored man respect himself, and then he would be
more respected by others. He lectured that the resolutions to be acted
upon by the end of the convention "would be unavailing, unless there
was action accordingly." In Clarke's concluding remarks, he said it was
a "mistake to suppose that the colored people of Massachusetts enjoyed
as many rights as their brethren in Canada." He also urged parents to
"send their sons out from the contaminating influences of large cities to
the wholesome atmosphere of agricultural districts." To young men, he
pressed "the importance of correct habits, temperance, and honorable
intercourse [relationships] with the opposite sex."[172]

Clarke established himself in Ontario and acquired several parcels
of land in East Sandwich, one of which was fifty-two acres in size.
While in Ontario, his commitment to the principles of the abolitionist
movement did not wane. In addition to farming, he utilized his property
to provide comfort and protection for escaped slaves from the United
States. One such slave was Jackson Whitney. While living on Clarke's
property, Whitney wrote to his former slave master, William Riley of
Springfield, Kentucky, in an attempt to appeal to Riley's "Christian
conscience" to free his wife and children. The letter was dated March
18, 1859. In reference to Clarke, Whitney explained with pride, "I

am comfortable situated in Canada, working for Geo. Harris [Lewis Clarke], one of the persons that act a part in *Uncle Tom's Cabin*. He was a slave a few years ago in Kentucky and now owns a farm so level that there are not hills enough on it to hide a dog, yet so large that I got lost in it the other day. He says that I may be the means of helping poor fugitives and doing them as much good as he does, in time."[173]

Whitney's letter was reprinted in several antislavery papers, including Garrison's *Liberator* and Lydia Child's *National Anti-Slavery Standard*. Clarke's site for runaway slaves sometimes numbered fifteen or more. During the years he lived in Canada, "a number of cabins were erected on his property and made it a sort of city of refuge for his fellow runaways."[174] Support for his project came from his personal resources as well as the industry of the fugitives. He often received revenue from antislavery contacts from across the border in the United States. Clarke said that in the winter he employed his protégées at wood chopping for the Detroit market, and the wood, delivered at that city, was worth just about what the expense of cutting had been. He described the runaways as "very delicate plants which a touch of frost wilted at once. They needed constant supervision for weeks after their arrival, before they could take care of themselves. They were in a measure helpless and could not realize their ability to look out for Number One, though they came to realize it in good time." The fugitives would often engage in religious discussions, which at times led to fights. The majority had religious backgrounds, which they felt obligated to defend. The arguments were usually between the Methodists and Baptists.[175]

While in Canada, Clarke became an accomplished farmer. He demonstrated his farming skills at the 1870 Essex County Fair in Windsor, Ontario. During the fair, he won more than half the exhibitor premiums. "Among his products were exaggerated cucumbers, overgrown cabbages, and pretentious potatoes. Lewis was the only exhibitor worthy of the name [premium], and as such the lion of the day." He also became a skilled weaver, which he learned from his Scottish father. At the same fair, he won first prize for spinning flax.[176]

Several years after Clarke established his residence in Canada, he married Emiline Bell Walker on December 8, 1859, in Detroit, Michigan.[177] Emiline was born on June 18, 1832, in Lexington, Kentucky. Her mother was owned by a Thomas Fowler who freed

Mrs. Walker and her two children, Emiline and Edmund. Edmund
Walker Sr., Emiline's father, was the slave of Henry Hart of Lexington.
Emiline's mother placed a mortgage upon herself and her children
to procure the money to buy Edmund Walker Sr.'s freedom. This
debt was paid from the wages Mr. Walker received as a janitor at
Transylvania College in Lexington and from the money Mrs. Walker
earned doing washing for students. The Walker family remained in
Lexington until racial persecution became so unbearable they decided
to move to Detroit. After two years, Mr. Walker was put in charge of a
manual labor school for blacks in Dawn, Ontario, Canada. The school,
located a short distance from Detroit and East Sandwich, may have
been the institution Lewis Clarke initiated through the Canadian-based
Agricultural, Mechanical, and Educational Association. Emiline spent
two years as her father's assistant at the school. After marrying Clarke,
Emiline moved to Clarke's farm on Pellett Road in East Sandwich. Nine
children were born to Emiline and Lewis between 1861 and 1872. One
of the children was Cyrus H. Clark, grandfather of the author, who was
born in 1863.

Josiah Henson, who lived near Lewis in Dawn, Ontario, was one
of the prototypes for Uncle Tom in Stowe's *Uncle Tom's Cabin.* The
friendship between Lewis and Josiah went back many years, beginning
in Kentucky. Henson described Clarke as a "white slave" because he was
at least three parts white. He proudly declared that "Lewis traveled and
lectured with me in the New England states. He is a very ingenious and
intelligent man, as Mrs. Stowe represented him…" as George Harris [in
Uncle Tom's Cabin.] In discussing Lewis's stay in Canada, Henson said
there was "great prejudice in certain localities in Canada against those
with even with one drop of black blood in their veins." Clarke's children,
according to Henson, experienced considerable discrimination when
Lewis attempted to enroll them in schools where white children were
taught. Henson said such was the case even though blacks paid "their
proportion of taxes and school rates."[178] Clarke confirmed Henson's
remarks about discrimination in Canada by stating in an interview
"Fugitives there have been subject to all sorts of impositions at the hands
of unprincipled Canadians." [179]

The first few years Lewis was in Canada, his financial status
flourished through speaking engagements and the profits he made
with hired fugitive slaves who worked on his farm. Clarke continued

to teach relocated blacks farming skills. The Civil War worked to his disadvantage financially when fugitive slaves were encouraged to leave Canada to fight for the Union. His financial fortunes had a positive turn after the war when he became an accomplished farmer. However, his life certainly was not as eventful compared to his many years of adventure and speaking to adoring crowds when he lived in the States. He likely became restless with his sedate Canadian lifestyle. As his children grew older and began entering school, the poor quality of Canada's education system also became a concern. Blacks were relegated to segregated schools at the time Clarke's children came of age in East Sandwich. The black schools were the lowest priority within the system, which negatively affected the programs.[180] Lewis also became increasingly concerned about Emiline's deteriorating health, which became more evident after the end of the Civil War. He began to feel the necessity to be close to Emiline's relatives in Oberlin and Lexington as her health grew worse. The accumulation of these concerns led Lewis to think seriously about returning to his roots in America.

Chapter 6

A Return To His Roots

Clarke sold all his Canadian land holdings and moved his family to Oberlin, Ohio, in 1874. The bulk of the money was to be used to educate his children. While in Oberlin the family lived on East College Street near Tappan Square, and there, Emiline passed away from consumption (tuberculosis) on February 22, 1876.[181] Living with the sorrow of Emiline's death, combined with the responsibility of raising young children as well as providing an adequate income for the family, must have been emotionally debilitating for the sixty-one-year-old Lewis.

For approximately five years following Emiline's death, Clarke traveled often on the lecture circuit while maintaining his home in Oberlin. During those years, Lewis held odd jobs such as "gardening and trimming trees. . . for the purpose of supporting and educating his children." He also had considerable sums of money given to him by friends who had taken an interest in his welfare. It was at this stage in his life, after assistance and encouragement from his friends, that he "expected to get out a history of his life and adventures."[182] From 1880 until his death, Clarke would mention often that he was working on a "history of his life"; however, no such manuscript has been located. While in Oberlin, Clarke attempted to raise his children as a single father while working; however, his good intentions faltered.

The 1880 Federal Census reflects that Clarke was sixty-five years old and resided in Oberlin, Lorain County, Ohio. Other members of the household were Matte A. Clark, age 19; Minnie E. Clark, age 18;

Cyrus N. Clark, age 17 (the author's grandfather); May L. Clark, age 15; Lewis E. Clark, age 13; Lettie [Violetta] C. Clark, age 11; John C. Clark, age 9; Willie R. Clark, age 9; Jennie R. Clark, age 8; John M. Walker, age 25, and Laura Walker, age 30.[183] The Walkers in the census were the brother and sister of Emiline, who cared for the children when Lewis was on the lecture circuit. The birthplace of all the children was reflected as Essex County in Ontario, Canada. Kentucky was indicated in the census as the birthplace for the Walkers and Lewis. The census does not include an e at the end of Clark. For unknown reasons, the 1880 census marks the beginning of future generations of the family dropping the e from Clarke.

In 1977 Virginia Clark Gayton, Lewis's granddaughter, was interviewed by a University of Washington archivist about Lewis. She recalled from her father, Cyrus, Lewis's oldest son, the circumstances in his home after Emiline's death in Oberlin. "The children were first raised by their aunt, Laura Walker, Emiline's younger sister, until some of the children found jobs, primarily in white families." She said from Cyrus's point of view, the children felt a sense of abandonment from their absentee father. Understandably the younger children had little appreciation or understandings of what Lewis had achieved on behalf of black people and the nation and were peeved by his absence while on speaking engagements.

Not all the siblings had the same impression of their father. As an example, the author's grandaunt Minnie Clarke Davis, Lewis's second-oldest child, spoke willingly and proudly about her father's place in history according to a reporter's observations in an April 1891 interview: "Mrs. Davis is a lady of refinement and culture, still young in years and in conversing with her it is difficult to imagine that her early days spent with her father in Canada was in daily touch as, you may say, with many of the great characters that once figured in the advance guard of that band of devoted spirits known as the early abolitionists." Minnie pointed out that Lewis's home was where "Douglass spent many of his early days, John Brown has walked, planned and plotted, to say nothing of scores of men of lesser lights once famous, but now, alas forgotten."[184]

In an 1886 letter Lewis sent to his old friend, the venerable abolitionist Reverend Austin Willey of Maine, he provides a more detailed picture of why he was away from his family so often. Lewis said he was called away to Kentucky "to do good there." He had planned to stay for three months; however, while speaking in the same region he lived as a slave, he was overcome by the heat and was sick for fifteen months. He remained there for three years. Clarke's sister-in-law, Laura Walker, who was looking after his children in Oberlin, assumed Clarke was dead and took the smaller children to Detroit to live in the home of Lewis's brother Cyrus. Clarke told Rev. Willey that he was in the process of bringing his younger children back to Oberlin for schooling. He ended his letter by saying that he was kindly treated throughout Kentucky and that his lectures were well attended.[185] Understandably, Clarke's children were distraught by his disappearance. It is interesting to note from *Detroit Free Press* newspaper accounts that Lewis made numerous visits to Detroit between 1876 and 1887 for speaking engagements. While there he resided at Cyrus's home. Clearly, Lewis maintained contact with his children but not on a continuous basis.

Lewis became more involved in the public arena advocating on behalf of former slaves. In May, 1876 he testified before the U. S. Congress Ways and Means Committee, for a bill that was considered to be of historical significance. The essence of the proposed legislation, which Clarke authored, was to allow blacks in Canada who had been refugees during slavery to return to the United States with their stock and farming elements without having to pay a duty. Lewis said the duty hindered the former slaves from purchasing farms in the Western and Southern states of America. Whether the bill passed is not clear.[186] Lewis's invitation to appear before a United States Congressional Committee after more than a twenty-year absence from America was a testament to his notoriety and influence. Following his testimony, Lewis was on retainer by a group of prosperous white planters in Kentucky led by Col. William Cassius Goodloe, who hired him to help build the black agricultural labor force in that state. Clarke's special emphasis was urging blacks not to migrate to the Northern states because he firmly believed there would be future economic opportunities for blacks in Kentucky. While working for the farmers, he maintained his home in Oberlin through the early 1880s but seldom lived there. During the time Clarke was working with black and white farmers, radical agrarianism was taking place, which drew the two racial groups together. This new phenomenon was emerging during the last two decades of the nineteenth century. The white Southern Farmer's Alliance and the Colored Farmers

Alliance became significant political entities when they began to see opportunities to come together on common farming interests. The Colored Alliance became the largest African American organization of the nineteenth century, comprising over one million black farmers, with members in every Southern state. "Under the tutelage of radical agrarian leaders, the white masses of the South were learning to regard the Negro as a political ally bound to them by economic ties and a common destiny. 'Never before or since have the two races in the South come so close together as they did during the Populist struggles.'"[187] The black and white farmers of the South became the foundation of the new Populist or People's party. The Populist Party sought the black vote in most of the Southern states. As the nineteenth century drew to a close, the white Populist leaders assumed that the Democrats in the South would attempt to disfranchise the Populists as well as their black allies in the Southern states. Political expediency led the Populist leadership to abandon the Colored Alliance and support disfranchisement of blacks throughout the South.[188] Because Clarke was heavily involved in the coming together of black and white farmers in Kentucky during the evolution of the Populist movement, it is understandable why, at the time, he felt so positive about the future of blacks in the South. Hard core apartheid in the South did not occur until the capitulation of the People's Party to the white Supremacy Democrats in the late 1890s.

Word of Lewis having a home in Oberlin was made known to a correspondent named Montgomery of the *Chicago Tribune* who interviewed Lewis in August 1880. His primary interest was Lewis's connection with *Uncle Tom's Cabin* as the prototype of George Harris. Fascinating aspects of the interview were the clarity of the sixty-five-year-old's responses and the consistency of his contention that the framework of the book directly matched the information he had supplied Harriet Beecher Stowe.

Clarke said that he had known Stowe for thirty-eight years, beginning when he lived with Stowe's in-laws in Cambridge, Massachusetts. When asked what points in *Uncle Tom's Cabin* he suggested to her, Lewis said, "Uncle Tom being whipped to death, incidents of my own life, the woman crossing the river on the ice, and numerous other incidents of slave life."

Other statements from Clarke in response to questions regarding key characters and circumstances were as follows:

"Is the statement of your history in the *Key to Uncle Tom's Cabin* correct?

"Yes."

"Who was Uncle Tom?"

"There were two characters of Uncle Tom. One was Josiah Henson, whom I know well. His history was that of Uncle Tom's throughout, but he did not undergo the tortures that Mrs. Stowe represents that he did . . ."

"Who was George Shelby?"

"His name was Robert Argo, a grandson of Simon Legree [Thomas Kennedy Sr.]. He is now living, and he remembers seeing a negro, Sam [Peter], a blacksmith, whipped to death by Legree, who sat in his room all the next day eating nothing, but drinking heavily of liquor. The picture of Uncle Tom's death was drawn from this circumstance."

"Were you ever at Josiah Henson's house and who was Chloe?"[189]

"Yes I was there quite often. Chloe was Henson's wife."

"Who was Wilson?"

"He was a Quaker; He met me at a hotel, as is related in Mrs. Stowe's narrative."

"What about the woman crossing the river on the ice [Eliza Harris]?"

"There was such a woman. She crossed the Ohio in 1841, the same winter I was in Oberlin. The river was full of floating cakes of ice at the time. She left one of her child's garments on the bank, so that those seeing it would think that she and her child had drowned. I knew quite well Lewis Coffin [famous abolitionist] and his wife, who gave her a change of clothing and cared for her after she landed." [Two acquaintances of Clarke at the time he escaped from Kentucky indicated in separate interviews that Clarke had a wife named Maggie, a.k.a., Margie, who was intimated to be the Eliza of the novel, but this was denied by Clarke.][190]

"Who was Tom Loker?"

"At the time I knew a young man named Henry Bibb, who went through just such perilous adventures [by shooting a slave catcher]."

"Who was Madame de Thoux?"

"She was my sister. The account given of her is generally correct. I still have a piece of the dress she wore while she lay chained in a New

Orleans slave-market. She was bought by a Mr. Coval, who took her on to Mexico and married her. My brother and a Mr. Lewis met her in New Orleans, and they brought the sleeve to me."

"Eva?"

"One of the Little Evas was Mary Ann Banton Logan. I saw her only a short time ago, while on a visit South, after forty years of absence. I ate dinner at her house and on her table I saw some spoons which I remembered seeing when I was a boy."[191]

Mrs. Logan and Clarke had the same grandfather, Captain Samuel Campbell. She was the daughter of John Banton and Elizabeth Campbell, Samuel Campbell's daughter. Letitia Campbell, his quadroon slave, was also his daughter and Clarke's mother. Although Mrs. Logan ultimately acknowledged being the prototype of Little Eva in Uncle Tom's Cabin, she did not want to accept Clarke's contention that Lewis's mother was Captain Campbell's daughter. "When Lewis told her [at dinner] that 'Little Eva' was the same Mary Banton he loved so dearly as a child, she was surprised, and amazed; but thanked Lewis for the lovely character he had given her." The lady who inspired the character Little Eva died in Elizabethtown, Kentucky, August 6, 1888, eight years after her last meeting with Lewis.[192]

Lewis's work on behalf of the Kentucky planters led to him making presentations in nearly every county in the state. Lewis was never harassed by whites during his travels, although there was the known presence of the Ku Klux Klan. He usually scheduled his appearances in the early afternoon to avoid the Klan, who usually committed their acts of violence at night. He talked about the past, present, and future of the Negro race and doubtless said many things that were distasteful to the mind-set of the former slave owners. Invariably harassers would attempt to bait Clarke with questions, such as where he felt better treated in comparing the North and the South. Ever the politician, Clarke would say to the Southerners he received better treatment in the South than in Chautauqua County, New York. (Much of what he said about his treatment in Busti was not an exaggeration.) During one presentation, an Irishman tried to pick a quarrel with him, questioning whether an Irishman or a Negro was the best under all circumstances and conditions. Clarke would say nothing more than that the man who held allegiance to the laws of his country and treated his neighbor as himself was the best citizen no matter what his nationality. He neutralized the agitator and simultaneously won the support of the crowd.[193] While in Kentucky, Lewis did not shy from being direct in his opinion of the ultraconservative Democrats, the political party in power at the time. In May of 1883, Lewis attended a Kentucky Republican Convention in Lexington. The Republican Party, being socially and politically progressive, was obviously the party of choice for Lewis. Asked to speak, he gave a typically witty Clarke presentation. During the course of his remarks, "he likened the Republican Party to a bushel of good beans with some bad ones among them and the Democratic Party as a bushel of bad beans with some good ones among them. Now of which bushel, he asked his colored brethren would they make their soup."[194]

Some may question how Lewis could go back to the South after all the misery he had experienced when he was a slave. The meeting in Kentucky with Mary Banton Logan, his cousin, was likely an attempt by Lewis to recreate a childhood he never had. Additionally, Mary Ann treated him kindly just as Little Eva treated George Harris in Mrs. Stowe's novel. The meeting of the aging celebrities of the great book came across as comforting to both. The years Lewis lived in the North were not altogether pleasant. Examples include the proslavery mob in Cambridgeport that destroyed the plates of his 1845 *Narrative* as well as Lewis's disingenuous relationships with Harriet Beecher Stowe and other abolitionists. His short stay in Busti, New York, was heart-wrenching. Catherine Storum, his wife, died a year after their marriage, which was followed by a property dispute with his widow's father. After Lewis recovered from his wife's death, he began to court the white sister of a fellow abolitionist he thought was a good friend. The man went into a rage because Clarke, a black man, dared to court his sister. The relationship broke off not only because of pressure from the woman's brother but from the community surrounding Busti. All of this resulted in the woman becoming a spinster. Racial prejudice in Canada was another factor why Lewis's family decided to move back to the States. Considering Lewis's negative experiences in the North and Canada, the South almost became a respite for him. In Kentucky, the people knew Lewis and he knew them. He associated with what he considered the "better class" of white people, who were straightforward with him. He knew where he stood. The hypocrisy and duplicity were not as ingrained into the culture in the South as it was in the North. He knew who his enemies were in the South; they were more difficult to identify in the North. The South created, for Lewis, a perverse kind of reassurance. Regardless, he expected to be treated with respect wherever he lived, which he would return in kind.

The Clarke family's journey back to the United States was at the cusp of the Great Exodus of African Americans from the South to the North after the withdrawal of Union troops from the South in 1876. The rises of the Ku Klux Klan, among other hate groups, resulted, followed by increased broad-based discriminatory actions against blacks. Within fourteen years after the troop withdrawal, more than three thousand blacks had been killed, largely at the hands of groups such as the Klan. During this period, thousands of Negroes had left their homes in the South, going in greatest numbers to Kansas, Missouri, and Indiana. Within twenty months, Kansas alone received forty thousand new black residents. Many ultimately ended up in the cities of those states or went back South because of the difficulties they encountered establishing farms.[195] Clarke was not the only black leader who wanted to stem the tide of the Exodus. Though Frederick Douglass was not entirely against the migration, he believed, however, that it was in the best interest of blacks to fight out this problem in the South; also he felt that the new movement would tend to aggravate conditions throughout the country. He warned that the Exodus was "an abandonment of the great and paramount principle of protection to person and property in every state of the Union." Blacks who remained leaders in the South, including Clarke, railed against the disappearance of communities and constituencies that still had some strength.[196]

Douglass said that the Exodus was a medicine, not a food. He went on to say that "[as a strategy] it is surrender, a premature, disheartening surrender, since it would make freedom and free institutions depend upon migration rather than protection; by flight, rather than right . . . it leaves the whole question of equal rights on the soil of the South open and still to be settled . . . it is a confession of the utter impracticability of equal rights and equal protection in any State, where those rights may be struck down by violence. Does not one exodus invite another, and in advocating one do we not sustain the demand for another?"[197]

Nationally, the majority of black leaders favored "reasonable migration." The black intelligentsia in the North, led by the venerable John Mercer Langston, who became the first president of Virginia State College and later a US congressman from Virginia, and Dr. Richard Greener, dean of Howard University School of Law, strongly favored the migration."[198] Greener publicly challenged the position of Douglass by stating that there was no future for Negroes in the South and that it was absurd to tell blacks to stick and fight it out when they had nothing to "fight it out with."[199] There were other political implications surrounding the migration. In 1879 the US Senate established a Select Committee to Investigate the Causes of the Removal of the Negroes from Southern States to the Northern States. Senator Daniel Voorhees, Democrat of Indiana, chaired the Committee. Senator Voorhees concluded that the emigration of blacks to the North was a Republican plot to tip his closely divided state in the 1880 presidential election. His fellow committee member, Senator Zebulon Vance, Democrat of North Carolina, viewed the mass migration as a planned threat to his state's supply of cheap labor. Senator Voorhees vowed, on the other hand, to "find out who these infernal damned political scoundrels are, who are trying to flood our State with a lot of worthless negroes." Obviously, the senator's remark was an ominous indicator of what blacks were to expect in Indiana as they sought refuge from the horrors of the South. The Voorhees committee's conclusions reflected the opinions of its chair.[200]

Clarke advocated, before the Civil War, that black slaves abandon the United States and move to Canada. Circumstances, however, had changed with the end of the war and the emancipation of the slaves. He believed that discrimination and racism existed throughout the nation in both the North and the South, but blacks had a better sense of dealing with their situation in the South because of their familiarity with the culture. If there had not been the threat of Clarke being sold to a less empathetic slave owner in Louisiana, he would have remained in Kentucky and not escaped to the North. History also shows us that the Exodus, over the long run, certainly was not the nirvana many black leaders expected. As the Northern city centers began to bulge with large populations of new black immigrants from the South, geographic racial hatred and prejudice became almost indistinguishable as the horrors of de facto and de jure discrimination spread throughout the nation particularly during the first half of the twentieth century. Lewis Clarke's rationale for encouraging African Americans not to rush to judgment about moving to the North was not about caving in to the apartheid South but to stand tall where they were born against those who would deny them their rights as citizens to "life, liberty, and the pursuit of happiness." Martin Luther King Jr. certainly embraced that kind of thinking when he led the Montgomery, Alabama, bus boycott in 1955, which triggered the modern-day civil rights movement. Finally, Martin Luther King's stand marked the beginning of the end of the migration. Nevertheless, challenges concerning the issues of race and class remain throughout the nation.

Clarke continued to travel throughout the United States well into his late seventies. He was an invited guest at various venues, delivering speeches about his past experiences as a slave, the abolitionist movement, temperance, and matters regarding the general plight of black people. Interspersed between these engagements, Clarke occasionally appeared at dime museums. Dime museums, at their inception, were educational, family-friendly entertainment sites, targeting a wide range of social classes. The museums were very popular during the latter part of the nineteenth century. Many of the museums, however, morphed into "freak shows" beginning in the early 1900s. As part of the dime museum's programming, traveling theatrical production companies of *Uncle Tom's Cabin* often performed and were very successful. Harriet Beecher Stowe had no copyright to prevent stage adaptations nor was she compensated. At one point, nearly five hundred "Tom companies" were offering productions around the country and remained popular more than fifty years after the publication of the novel. Some of the shows removed characters from the original book, enlarged roles of others, and added song and dance, even comedy, to conform the story to elements of the popular minstrel shows of the day. Toward the end of the nineteenth century, the actors and performers were often white in black makeup. As time went by, the shows became considerably more demeaning of blacks. On the stage, Uncle Tom was an old man—meek, submissive, desexualized, with no self-esteem—not the spiritually and morally enlightened hero of Stowe's novel who died defending other slaves. Regrettably, the understanding that the general public had about the character Uncle Tom and *Uncle Tom's Cabin* was driven more by the misleading stage productions than the book itself. Hence the epithet "He's an Uncle Tom" was directed toward condescending and meek blacks. Invariably, Clarke was the most famous of the real-life characters of the novel when he appeared in the productions. Lewis traveled with Rosco and Smith's *Uncle Tom's Cabin* troupe for a year and a half. His part in the shows was to speak a few lines and to spin on the linen wheel while in character as George Harris.[201] Not much acting was required on the part of Lewis because he and George Harris were fundamentally one and the same. Clarke often appeared at the dime museums individually as the famous personality he was, the George Harris of *Uncle Tom's Cabin*. He would demonstrate his skills on the spinning wheel and regale the audiences with his real-life story as a slave. At the end of each performance, Lewis would pass out photographs of himself sitting beside a spinning wheel. A February 1891 article by a reporter in Lexington, Kentucky, indicated that "he [Clarke] has been in many of the most prominent museums in the United States."[202]

While in Philadelphia for a speaking engagement in 1890, Clarke said in an interview, "In the museums, *Uncle Tom's Cabin* show, and selling my pictures I have managed to collect something and that will be used in giving my last boy a good education."[203] As the shows became more demeaning, Clarke said, "Probably when I went into museums some people had a curiosity to see me, and to those who spoke to me, I told them that I had turned out to be a big monkey." His pride would no longer allow him to participate in what was becoming charade. Obviously the speaking engagements by themselves gave Lewis the opportunity to tell his life story comfortably and with dignity.[204]

In the late 1880s, Lewis left Oberlin for good to reside in Lexington after his children found jobs or continued to live with other family members in Oberlin as well as other cities around the country. Lewis bought a rundown home in Lexington, fixed it up, sold it, and "made sufficient on that to keep him going for a while." He then began boarding in the city. Clarke, at seventy-six years old, was observed as mentally sharp and vigorous. He demonstrated that he "possessed a most retentive memory, recalling with exactness, scenes and incidents of the occurrences of his early history, which has been filled with much that was perilous and exciting." Daisy Fitzhugh, a reporter for *Frank Leslie's Illustrated Newspaper,* saw Clarke as "a striking, picturesque looking man of seventy-six, with a refined face, silken snow-white locks, that curl about his head, and skin of Caucasian fairness."[205] He weighed about 175 pounds, and stood five feet eight inches in height, showing that at one time he was a model of physical manhood. His personality and the way that he carried himself led one to feel to be in the presence of a person "who was not a stranger to good society and culture."[206] For at least the early part of the 1890s, his relatively good health and clear mind allowed him to travel extensively after leaving Oberlin. A further indication of his high level of energy—Clarke said after a speech in the summer of 1890 at the Nineteenth Street Baptist Church in Washington, DC, that he was on his way to Kentucky, Minnesota, Nebraska, Illinois, and Ohio for multiple presentations in each state as well as New York City and Philadelphia. His appearances in those areas of the country were primarily held at black churches, but he was also invited to speak at gatherings in cities sponsored by such organizations as the Women's Union Christian Association, the Afro-American League, and the Home for Destitute Colored Girls, among many others. A common comment made by those who were present at his lectures observed, "Any person who has read the story of *Uncle Tom's Cabin,* and doubtless there are few who have failed to do so, will remember 'George Harris,' the persecuted and hard worked slave, who finally made a bold dash for freedom and was successful in securing and afterwards enjoying his liberty."[207]

Clarke's extensive traveling began to wind down in the early 1890s. He had his last contact with his brother Milton in the spring of 1891 when he spent several months with him in Cambridge, Massachusetts. While residing with Milton, Lewis provided one his most revealing interviews to a reporter with the *Boston Globe.* The interviewer, Robert T. Teamoh, more than anyone previously, was able to print more insights into Clarke's character, wisdom, and indeed, his legacy than any other writer. Clarke was also more likely open to the interview because Teamoh was black. In later years, Teamoh became a notable figure in his own right as a businessman and politician in the Boston area. Clarke began the conversation by telling Teamoh that he was giving him information that had never appeared in print and that much of it was in a manuscript about his life, which Clarke apparently gave him. Clarke, the ever-staunch Lincoln Republican, jokingly told Teamoh he would be more revealing to him because he liked the enterprise of the *Boston Globe,* even though it was a Democratic newspaper. He went on to say, "I travel about the country lecturing on *Uncle Tom's*

Cabin, and sometimes I show how I used to work the spinning wheel. I want my work to be a history of the times that have passed. You and your generation and those who are coming after you can never know or feel what we who have been slaves endured. You are surrounded by golden opportunities such as I never dreamed would come. Ah! As I look back and think of the real condition of them, and today see my people rushing forward and helping with might and main the fast turning wheels of this now free republic, I cannot help but shed tears of thankfulness. I guess you have got enough, but before I close I want to add that after the Fugitive Slave Law had been passed an effort was made to stop the abolition papers throughout the country, and *Uncle Tom's Cabin* was denounced in the severest terms. But such a work it was needed, and it greatly helped the cause. The only fault I had with it was that it did not tell in language strong enough, the woes of the slaves who were branded with hot irons, starved, whipped, trampled upon and otherwise cruelly treated. I have come to the conclusion that, after all, the colored man in this country has been placed here for some purpose. What it is I do not know, but the future will reveal. I have great faith in the rising generations of my race."

His interview with Teamoh emphasized African Americans knowing and appreciating the evolution of our history. He also expressed the importance of perseverance in challenging continuing injustices against our people. The essence of his message was what we hear from many black preachers on Sunday mornings: "We are not where we want to be, we are not where we ought to be, but thank God we are not where we were." As a person, Lewis Clarke came through as a wise, compassionate, and prescient human being. This was reflected in his prediction, "I have great faith in the rising generations of my race. Let us not be judged by a quarter of a century; give us 50 years and then we will show what we are going to be." Lewis's vision takes us to the cusp of the Civil Rights movement, including the GI Bills of 1944 and 1952; the *Brown v. Board of Education* Supreme Court decision of 1954; the Montgomery Bus Boycott of 1955; and the emergence of the Reverend Martin Luther King. All of the aforementioned laid the groundwork for the passage of the landmark Civil Rights Act of 1964.[208] A constant character trait of Lewis's life was being proactive rather than reactive to the social, political, and economic challenges that faced African Americans. He was a victim of the institution of slavery, which was entrenched in American culture for over three hundred years. Nevertheless, he envisioned its ultimate demise and worked every day of his adult life to make that happen. He then looked ahead fifty years and visualized levels of achievement of his people that he never dared to imagine while enslaved. Clarke's combination of enlightened vision and committed implementation give food for thought for leaders of any future period of history.

Clarke was a profoundly proud black man. He did not equivocate. He said as much the day before his interview with Mr. Teamoh, in a speech at the St. Paul AME Church in Cambridge. "In infancy I was cruelly dragged from my mother's arms. I was sold into the next county. Since then I have been sold to pay off a mortgage at the price of $1,250. *When I came north I found that there was a disposition to apologize for slaveholders and I fought against it. I have since took my freedom and used my complexion as a means to an end. With this complexion I have never yet disavowed my race. I say this with pride!"* Looking back, his concluding remarks at St. Paul's continue to be relevant to this day and, in some respects, are a dream deferred for much of black America: "I am happy tonight in my old age to see what a free man is doing and to you young people I say that the main point of progress is in the family. To parents I say, set no example which a child cannot safely follow. It will not be a great while before some of the states South will be in the hands of the descendants of slaves. A remarkable progress we are making there. We are getting hold of and keeping the land."[209]

He may have been too sanguine with this remark. However, it reflected a fundamental element of his character in that he firmly believed the inevitability that America would continue to provide opportunities for his people to achieve even greater heights.

Chapter 7

Tumultuous Twilight Years

By the mid 1890s, Clarke was physically feeble and also faced financial difficulties. He had a severe case of the grippe and was scarcely able to move about. He had a little home at Fifty-Seven Race Street in Lexington, Kentucky that he built, the rent of which he was able to pay his board. In 1894, his tenant ran off without paying his rent, and subsequently, the home burned down. The meager insurance that he had was not enough to rebuild the house, so he had to go into debt to have a roof over his head. He was living in the home alone with only a bed and three chairs. Lewis might have died in obscurity if not for earthshaking events that took place in 1895.

Perhaps the most publicity Clarke ever received resulted from an insult by a Lexington, Kentucky city employee, which Clarke, because of his pride, would probably have preferred to let pass by. Clarke applied to vote in Lexington on registration day in May of 1895, but because of his race he was denied by a city clerk. The incident came to the attention of a young newspaper correspondent in the city, R. L. McClure, who was told that Clarke was the "prototype" of George Harris, the character in Mrs. Stowe's famous novel *Uncle Tom's Cabin*. McClure contacted Clarke, who revealed to him his financial and health circumstances. The old gentleman went on to say, "Yes, I am trying to live in my little house, but I have scarcely anything to live upon. . . It seems strange to me that I, who have handled thousands of dollars and traveled from one end of the United States to the other, should in my old age be an object of charity and possessed of nothing with which to keep the wolf from the door. When I was making money I used every dollar of it to forward the cause I espoused fifty-four years ago."[210] McClure questioned Lewis further about his financial status. He was asked specifically whether he received any compensation from Harriet Beecher Stowe as a result of the vast amount of information he provided her for the writing of *Uncle Tom's Cabin*. He replied, "I never got a cent from it. The only benefit that I received was the advertisement [publicity] it gave me." From his cryptic response, one can detect a tinge of anger and bitterness. Clarke never spoke disparagingly of Stowe in terms of what the book accomplished. He was always effusive in his praise for her in that regard. No record indicates Clarke ever asked Stowe for compensation; however, the fact that she did not offer peeved him.[211]

McClure's story on Clarke appeared on the front page in Lexington's the *Press-Transcript* on November 23, 1895 with the heading "Pitiful Is the Condition of Lewis George Clarke,The Original Uncle Tom." The headline, although inaccurate in stating that Clarke was the Uncle Tom in Mrs. Stowe's book rather than George Harris, set the tone for a controversy that swept the country. "One of the saddest cases ever known in Lexington is that of Lewis George Clark, better known as George Harris. He is in absolutely destitute circumstances and although nearly eighty-four [eighty] years old is without the necessities of life to carry him through the approaching winter. He is a historic character, being none other than the original of Harriet Beecher Stowe's *Uncle Tom's Cabin*. The old man is very feeble . . . scarcely able to go about . . . and in a despondent mood."[212]

Within less than two weeks of McClure's story, a letter under the name of Harriet Beecher Stowe was sent out to key newspapers within the United States that printed the letter. Special focus was on parties in Lexington in which she said, "The man you speak of, George Lewis Clarke, who is going about representing himself to be the original George in *Uncle Tom's Cabin* does so at his own presumption. I never saw the man, and don't remember ever having even heard of him, although I have before received letters telling of various individuals who were going about the country representing themselves to be the originals of Uncle Tom, or George Harris, as the case might be. Neither he nor any other man stood for the character of George Harris, who was a creature of my own brain—probable but not living character."[213] Reaction to Mrs. Stowe's protestations was just as swift. A woman from

Ashtabula County, Ohio, wrote to the Lexington *Press Transcript* on December 1, 1895:

> The enclosed taken from the *Cleveland World* leads me to write to you that Lewis Clark therein mentioned is truthful, and if he needs any proof of his character as an honest man he can easily secure it among Northerners, who have known him ever since he escaped from slavery. My father, Philander Winchester, befriended him and also cut the ropes from the arms of a brother of Lewis [Milton] and set him free as Lewis will tell you if you only say Winchester to him . . .
>
> Yours Respectfully, Etta D. Winchester Fitch

Mrs. Fitch refers to the highly publicized attempt of two bondsmen from Kentucky to capture escaped slaves Lewis and his brother Milton outside Oberlin, Ohio, in 1842. The reporter who covered the incident for the *Philanthropist Newspaper* was Harriet Beecher Stowe using the pseudonym Franklin.

Lewis's truthfulness was also verified in a revealing December 2, 1895, article in the *Boston Globe*, "True Incident from Which Mrs. Stowe Gave 'George Harris' and 'Eliza' to the Reading World." Professor S. G. W. Rankin, son of the famous Presbyterian abolitionist John Rankin, substantiated Lewis Clarke's story regarding Harriett Beecher Stowe's character Eliza in *Uncle Tom's Cabin*. He felt compelled to defend Clarke on the heels of the worldwide dispatches in 1895 concerning statements by Mrs. Stowe accusing Clarke of being a fraud. Professor S. W. G. Rankin was speaking to a church audience in Hartford, Connecticut, on November 29, 1895. Professor Rankin confirmed the conversation Clarke had with his father in 1842, in Oberlin, Ohio, regarding Eliza of the novel. Professor Rankin reflected that an 1891 interview Clarke had regarding his father and Eliza was the factual truth when he said, "A woman along with her child was chased across the ice of the Ohio River by slave catchers. One of the women who helped to put dry clothes on 'Eliza' after her escape was alive in 1891. Her name was Laura Haviland and lived at that time in Englewood near Chicago. She was known as 'Rachel the Halliday the Quaker Lady' in the novel. Levi Coffin the abolitionist of Cincinnati was Phineas the Quaker who assisted 'Eliza.'"

Clarke went on to say that Reverend Rankin was a strong abolitionist, and "one night [in Oberlin] we were relating adventures and he told me the story of the woman who was pursued by hounds with a babe on her breast boldly leaping across the blocks of ice on the Ohio River to gain freedom. Her name I do not remember. She was sent on to freedom."[214] The conversation Clarke had with John Rankin concerning Eliza was in the winter of 1842, nearly ten years before Stowe wrote her book. The story was, in turn, passed on to Harriet by Clarke during their conversations at the home of the Saffords, her in-laws. In Stowe's *Key to Uncle Tom's Cabin,* chapter 5 on Eliza, Stowe relates the following: "With regard to the incident of Eliza's crossing the river on the ice—as the possibility of the thing has been disputed—the writer gives the following circumstance in confirmation. Last spring, while the author [Stowe] was in New York, a Presbyterian clergyman of Ohio [obviously Reverend Rankin] came to her, and said, 'I understand they dispute that fact about the woman's crossing the river. Now, I know all about that, for I got the story from the very man that helped her up the bank. I know it is true, for she is now living in Canada.'" Stowe contended she got the information about Eliza crossing the Ohio River from Rankin no earlier than 1852. Clarke, on the other hand, stated unequivocally that he got the information about Eliza in 1842 from Reverend Rankin before he became a resident of the home of Harriett Beecher Stowe's sister-in-law Mary Safford. Clarke also contends that he related the Eliza story to Mrs. Stowe during her interviews with him in the 1840s, years before the publication of *Uncle Tom's Cabin.* Reverend Rankin's son supported Clarke's version of the story, which on its face is more credible.[215]

Lewis received letters from throughout the country expressing regret for his financial woes but very little money to assist him. Clarke's pride would not allow him to ask for handouts. As a result of his financial circumstances and array of illnesses, one would have expected a flow of funds on his behalf. The full-bore assault against Clarke's veracity by the Stowe family certainly had a negative impact. A cogent letter in support of Clarke came from an anonymous New Yorker to the *Boston Transcript:*

To the Editor of the *Transcript*: When I read in the *Transcript* this Saturday evening the account of Lewis Clark claiming to be the original George Harris of "Uncle Tom's Cabin." The name seemed familiar so I took down the *"Key to Uncle Tom's Cabin"* by Harriet Beecher Stowe and read chapter four of the book.

The New Yorker went on to indicate that from the book, Stowe knew Lewis Clarke and related for over two double-spaced pages about Clarke's escape from slavery and reaching Canada etc. These were all matters reflected in Clarke's *Narrative* as well as speeches and interviews for over fifty years. The reader went on to point out that Mrs. Stowe's letter in the *Transcript* declared that she never saw Clarke before and had never heard of him. He went on to say,

It is possible that Lewis Clark of Kentucky is a different person than the one of whom Mrs. Stowe wrote. But in that case it is a little singular that Miss Stowe in her letter did not refer to the coincidence of names, and distinctly state that while a Lewis Clark was one of the originals from which her mother drew the character of "George Harris," yet the present claimant is not that man.

It occurs to the writer that there may possibly be another solution of the question. It is forty-three years since Mrs. Stowe published *Uncle Tom's Cabin*, and forty-two years since she published the *Key to Uncle Tom's Cabin*; and she is now eighty-three years old, an age at which the memory of many persons becomes defective; and then if I am not mistaken, it has been published again and again during several years past that the mind of Mrs. Stowe is not now clear and vigorous as it was in her earlier days. May it not be then that the existence of Lewis Clarke, and of his being one of those from whom she drew the character of "George Harris," may have passed from her mind; and thus Lewis Clarke of Kentucky may still be the man of whom Mrs. Stowe wrote in her book?

[Signed] W. H., New York, December 4, 1895.[216]

WH of New York was accurate in his assessment of Mrs. Stowe's mental state. She had suffered a significant mental decline in 1889 that left her with diminished faculties. An admirer wanted to send Stowe a signed copy of a treasured document, but Mrs. Stowe's daughter, Hattie [Harriet], discouraged it. She explained that she was not able to appreciate the gesture due to the fact that "intellectually she is not now above a child of two or three years." Hattie lamented that "her mind is in a strange state of childishness and forgetfulness with momentary flashes of her old self that come and go like falling stars."[217] Harriet Beecher Stowe's failing mental state toward the end of her life has been clearly documented. Stowe never recovered from her mental decline. She was described as "forgetful," had "limited power of concentration," "intellectually . . . not above a child of two or three," and years before her life had ended, her "brain . . . gave out."[218]

After receiving the dispatch from Lexington about Clarke, the *World*, out of empathy for the old gentleman, wrote in an editorial that the paper would receive funds on Clarke's behalf and forward the money to him. The *Sun* followed with this headlined story:

Mrs. H. B. Stowe Never Saw Clark.

The World Promoting His False Pretense That He Is George Harris.

The World of this city on Sunday contained a long article about Lewis Clark of Lexington, Kentucky who claims to be the original George Harris of *Uncle Tom's Cabin*. It stated that a reporter had visited him at his home and found him at the advanced age of eighty-four, unable to work, and on the verge of starvation. The supposed 'George Harris' told his story in part as follows.

The *Sun* article went on to reiterate the information in the Lexington dispatch and then remarked,

The whole story was carefully written for effect and was accompanied by the editorial announcement that funds for the relief of Mr. Clark would be received and forwarded by *The World*.

A letter to the author of *Uncle Tom's Cabin* as to the truth of Mr. Clark's statements brought the following reply from her [Harriet Beecher Stowe's] daughter:

Hartford, Conn. Dec. 3, 1895 Dear Sir: Your letter of inquiry relating to the man who calls himself the original George Harris of *Uncle Tom's Cabin* reached my mother, Mrs. Stowe, last evening. I write to say that my mother never saw the man, or even heard of him, until two years ago, when she received a letter from the West stating that a man by the name of Lewis Clark, claiming to be the original George Harris, was exhibiting himself as such in dime museums, and enclosing also a picture with long account of him taken from some number of Frank Leslie's Illustrated Weekly, in 1891, which was entirely untrue from beginning to end, so far as it had any connection with my mother or her writing *Uncle Tom's Cabin*

(Signed) Miss H. B. Stowe.

The *Sun* concluded the story with the admonition, "Mr. Clark's claims with *the World's* endorsement for the appeal for a relief fund amounts to practically that, has been given wide publicity. The imposition promoted by *The World* should be effectively checked by Miss Stowe's authoritative letter."[219] A sidelight to the battle between the two publications was that in the same year, 1895, William Randolph Hearst purchased the *New York Journal* and subsequently drew many writers away from Joseph Pulitzer's *New York World*. Was it possible that the insightful WH referred to previously was none other than the king of "yellow journalists" himself? If so, was he fanning the flames to help position his new publication for a better business advantage in the circulation war that was taking place in the city? [220]

Harriet Beecher Stowe and/or her surrogates would not let the Clarke matter fade away. The *Sun* reported that after Mrs. Stowe's daughter's letter discounting Clarke appeared in their paper, "telegrams as thick as fleas" came to their offices from whites in Lexington and other parts of Kentucky supporting Clarke's assertions. The *Sun* and Stowe felt compelled to respond again, this time with Harriett Beecher Stowe signing the communication herself. *"The Sun* is in possession of additional testimony upon the point which must end this controversy. In a statement, dated December 8, Harriet Beecher Stowe, the author of *Uncle Tom's Cabin*, writes: 'I again assert, as I have already stated, that the characters of Uncle Tom and George Harris had no living prototype, but were created by me. (signed) Harriet Beecher Stowe.'"

The *New York Sun* responded again: "This statement ends the whole matter. *The World* has only one honest course to pursue: to return the money its readers have sent to it for their pretender, and acknowledge, as gracefully as it may, that it has imposed on the public. To do otherwise will be obtaining money under false pretenses."[221] *The Sun* made no reference to her rapidly declining memory and general mental state, which had been corroborated at least five years before the article was written. Under pressure, the *World* backed away from Clarke, accepted the word of Mrs. Stowe, notified the public of the newspaper's "error," and refunded the money sent to them for Clarke.[222]

The New York newspapers, inconceivably, gave Mrs. Stowe a free pass on the matter. WH's rational suggestion to simply examine the facts and then ask Mrs. Stowe to defend them could have solved the controversy. Two of the most powerful newspapers in the world were so intimidated by Stowe's lofty status they in essence said to their readers, "The facts be damned—Mrs. Stowe said the Negro lied. That is all we need to know." The positions by the New York newspapers concerning the controversy was not a sterling moment in the history of the free press in America.

Clearly, Stowe and her daughter lied. Mrs. Stowe contradicted what she had written about Clarke in the *Key to Uncle Tom's Cabin* in 1853. Both the *New York Sun* and *the World* were presented the facts by individuals who knew Clarke in Lexington as well as the writings in the *Key*. The reasons why they stood by Stowe, although sordid, are clear from political and commercial interests of the times. She held sacrosanct status in the North because of her book and its impact against slavery.

She was also seen as a strong Christian and devoted mother as well as a preeminent world advocate for human rights. Whose word should one believe that of a poor eighty-year-old ex-slave or the iconic Harriet Beecher Stowe? The New York newspapers evidently concluded that because of Stowe's popularity and influence in the North, siding with Clarke would not be commercially advantageous.

The continuing denunciation of the powerless former slave by Mrs. Stowe reminds one of Shakespeare's insightful line "The lady doth protest too much." Stowe's flood of letters to the press did indeed lead newsmen in Lexington as well as other publications in the South to become more curious about the truth of the matter. The general feeling of white Southerners was reflected in a headline in the *Richmond, Times:* "A Parallel for Mrs. Stowe. The Veracity of the Author of Uncle Tom's Cabin Is Imperiled. Is Lewis Clarke 'George Harris'? In a Book Written by Mrs. Stowe and Published in 1853 she said the Negro Lewis Clarke Was an Acquaintance of Hers, and Now She Denies Ever Having Seen or Heard of Him." The *Richmond Times* article included denial letters from Stowe as well as the statement from the *New York World* accepting the "evidence" from Mrs. Stowe as conclusive. The *Richmond Times*, however, sided with Clarke. The Richmond paper made clear what Stowe wrote about Clarke in *The Key:* "Lewis Clarke is an acquaintance of the writer. Soon after his escape from slavery he was received into the family of a sister-in-law of the author, and there educated. His conduct during this time was such as to win for him uncommon affection and respect, and the author has frequently heard him spoken of in the highest terms by all who knew him. His conduct during this time was as such as to win for him uncommon affection and respect . . . The gentleman in whose family he so long resided says of him in a recent letter to the writer: 'I would trust him as the saying is, with untold gold' . . . It was also reflected in the *Key* and reiterated in the *Richmond Times* that incidents in Clarke's life were 'Personally related by him to the author.'"[223]

The *Richmond Times* article concluded by quoting J. Henning Helms, a prominent white resident of Lexington who conducted a detailed investigation of Clarke's background, researching the *Key to Uncle Tom's Cabin* and personally interviewing Lewis. He said that Clarke was "neither a fraud nor a fake." He went on to say, "I neither know nor care whether Mrs. Stowe's purpose in defaming Clarke was malicious."[224] In a separate interview at the time, Clarke responded in a resigned manner, "Well, I am too old now to get benefit from lying, and as she is crazy, it can't be expected that she would remember that far back as that, but every meeting I had with Mrs. Stowe is as fresh in my mind as if it were yesterday."[225]

Generally, Southerners hated *Uncle Tom's Cabin* and how they were portrayed by Mrs. Stowe. They reveled in the fact that Stowe was being called, at best, a prevaricator by the prototype of one of the main characters in the book. Although Southerners researched and publicly verified Clarke's claims, there certainly were political motives behind their support of Lewis. James "Polk" Miller, a former Confederate soldier from Virginia who became a well-known entertainer after the Civil War, got "embroiled in the national controversy." Miller was also known as a "celebrated delineator of negro dialect and interpreter of Negro character." He traveled the country with a black singing quartet, which was unusual for a white man to do in those days; and sang and played on his banjo "authentic negro songs." This led to Miller's strange assumption that he could determine better than most anyone whether Clarke was telling the truth. In promoting himself, Polk added that he had studied Negro character his whole life and was familiar with every chapter of Mrs. Stowe's great novel. Miller was in Lexington during the peak of the controversy and was asked by a prominent local citizen to determine Clarke's veracity: "On December 5, 1895 Miller interviewed the aging gentleman, quizzing him on matters pertaining to the characters and decided unequivocally that Clarke was who he claimed to be." Polk's interview stressed the callous stinginess of Northerners, i.e., abolitionists, including Stowe, who used Clarke's life story as a call to arms. Polk emphasized that since it was made known that Clarke was ill and in dire financial circumstances, he "daily received mail from Northern well-wishers. The missives very seldom contained money." Polk failed to mention whether funds came from Southerners. Polk took advantage of Lewis's despondent state by interpreting from Clarke "that he had fled slavery for fear of being separated from his master who he loved dearly, and that the people of the South are the greatest friends of the Negro." What led Polk to declare such a specious assumption is not clear. Polk apparently did not want to recognize that Lewis devoted his entire adult lifetime against all vestiges slavery, especially the role of slave owners.[226]

On November 30, 1895, a reporter from the Lexington, Kentucky, *Leader* interviewed Clarke while he was in the colored department of the Protestant Infirmary in the city and baited him with the question, "Well, Uncle George, the pangs of poverty are more bitter than the yoke of slavery, are they not?" The physically crippled old gentleman looked grave for a moment as he answered retrospectively, "Oh, no it is not so bad as that. Physical want is hard enough, but in its worst form it is sweeter than the want for human liberty." His response to the reporter was consistent with his view of slavery for his entire life. The reporter expected a response similar to what Polk interpreted that Clarke said to him. At least this Southern reporter quoted Lewis as he responded.[227]

The battle of arms between the North and the South ended in 1865, but the war of words continued thirty years later. The cub reporter in Lexington who initially wrote the dispatch about Clarke's status certainly did not anticipate the ensuing conflict between Clarke and Mrs. Stowe. He merely wanted to explain the sad condition of a once well-known black citizen of the Lexington community. Newspapers began to choose sides after the Stowe family covered the nation with press releases and letters denying Clarke's story. Ironically Southern newspapers, especially those in Lexington, arose to defend their local black hero against the Northern press in "liberal" New York City, which gave unequivocal support to Mrs. Stowe. Fifty-five years earlier, when Clarke was living in Cambridge, he was generally recognized in a positive manner in publications in cities throughout the Northeast as a result of his exploits. The public would have understood why Mrs. Stowe did not remember Clarke in 1895 because of her mental condition. However, she and her representatives never commented on her published remarks about Clarke in *A Key to Uncle Tom's Cabin*. Additionally, Stowe, before she had symptoms of dementia and loss of memory, rejected Clarke's request for a letter to state he had given her some of the incidents in the book. She instead verbally acknowledged to him that he did. The cover-up by Stowe was exposed by the Southern press through the revelations discovered in the *Key*. A strange phenomenon is that few, if any, recognized biographers of Mrs. Stowe make mention in their publications of what was regarded by the news media at the time as a national controversy. Facts revealed here justify further research in order to provide more detailed information and a clearer perspective of the impact Lewis Clarke had on the writing of one of the greatest novels ever written. Indications are that such research would enhance the stature of an important figure in antebellum American history.

Harriet Beecher Stowe died on July 1, 1896, two weeks before her eighty-fifth birthday. A month later the Lexington press reported that "Lewis Clarke who gave Mrs. Stowe the information from which she wrote the greater part of her famous novel, *Uncle Tom's Cabin* . . . was overcome by heat . . . and picked up by an ambulance. His condition is critical . . . The denial of his identity by Mrs. Stowe just before her death has banished every hope he had of receiving aid from his friends in the north." The report was accurate regarding the lack of funds coming from the North. Also, Mrs. Stowe's searing denunciations of him certainly had a harmful impact on his integrity as well as his legacy.[228]

The story of the destitute hero spread throughout the world. The *Lexington Leader* felt compelled to defend its community and, indeed, the state of Kentucky by writing, "Lewis Clarke's destitution has been the occasion of a number of adverse criticisms in foreign papers upon the charity of Kentuckians and Lexingtonians, and especially of his own race. Injustice to the people of this city and State be it said that few remembered that Clark lived here, and none were aware of his abject poverty and destitution."[229] Although the statement by the *Leader* was honorable, it is a stretch of the imagination to believe that it would have been made if wide exposure of Clarke's condition had not taken place.

A citizen of New Zealand untainted by the politics and phobias of race in America saw the dispatch about Clarke in the *Otago Daily Times* in Dunedin, New Zealand. Charles Umbers, a well-known philanthropist in New Zealand, took a humanitarian interest in Clarke's predicament and communicated by letter with the Mayor of Lexington, Joseph B. Simrall. He asked him if the statements in the dispatch about Clarke were true. The letter was turned over by the mayor to D. T. Baxter, a reporter acting as the mayor's pressman, to respond to Mr. Umbers. Baxter gave a detailed account of Clarke's life to Umbers and that, indeed, Lewis Clarke, the original George Harris in Mrs. Stowe's book, was living in Lexington in destitute circumstances, was very infirm, and was being vouched for by reputable citizens in the United States.[230] After receiving confirmation from by Baxter, Umbers decided to promote an entertainment fund-raiser in his hometown, Dunedin, for the benefit of Clark. On October 2, 1896, Mr. Umbers held a benefit musical engagement for Lewis in Garrison Hall, the leading opera house in Dunedin, which was filled to overflowing. A feature of the concert was the revival of favorite old-time Negro melodies and English ballads.

After the concert it was reported that "Lewis George Clark[e] has probably never been seen by any one of the vast audience at the benefit. His claim upon the public sympathy, beyond the fact that he was the original of a well-known character in a touching and successful novel, consists in his being poor and old, but he lives far from New Zealand—in Lexington, Kentucky—so that there was no apparent reason why the people of Dunedin should be more than the people of any other place outside of the United States, take a special interest in this case."[231] Mr. Umbers sent the proceeds from the concert, $350, to Mayor Simrall, with the money reaching him sometime in March of 1897. The money was used by the mayor in making the last days of the "grand old man" as comfortable as possible. It saved him from going to the poorhouse, a fate that he dreaded. After the money arrived, Clarke moved from the Protestant Infirmary where he was staying when word of his condition was publicized and began rooming at the home of Harrison and Rhoda Richardson at 198 East Fifth Street in Lexington.[232]

Before the money from Mr. Umbers could reach Lewis, his last known public appearance before his death took place in January 1897: "The first parade of Salter & Martin's *Uncle Tom's Cabin* Company with old Lewis Clark, the original George Harris of Harriett Beecher Stowe's famous book, created a profound sensation at Frankfort, Kentucky, and the streets were crowded long before he came out driving a pony in the parade. He recently joined the show at Lexington." Clarke was eighty-two years of age at the time and was obviously highly regarded, particularly by the older citizens of this old Southern town. Although he had trepidations about appearing in such shows, the cold fact was that he had limited income options. Nevertheless, it was also clear he could not resist the adulation of the crowd. The response from the spectators must have warmed his heart, reminding him of the bygone days of the antislavery movement when thousands would cheer his oratory.

Clarke died less than a year from the date of the parade[233] on Friday December 16, 1897, in Lexington, not far from where he was born. The front-page article about his demise in the *Lexington Herald* was entitled "FINISHED—The Life of George Lewis Clark Comes to a Close with Evening.—AN HISTORIC NEGRO—He Was the Prototype of the George Harris in the Story of *Uncle Tom's Cabin*—REMARKABLE CAREER ENDS." The article began, "George Lewis Clark is dead. The end came peacefully at 4:15 o'clock yesterday afternoon while the old man lay asleep at the place where he boarded on Fifth Street. He was in his eighty-sixth [eighty-second] year, and his death was due to infirmities of his advanced age."[234]

Clarke's funeral took place in Lexington at St. Paul's African Methodist Episcopal Church on Sunday afternoon, December 18, 1897, at two o'clock. By order of Republican Governor, William Bradley of Kentucky, the body of Clarke laid in state at the city's auditorium. This was the first time in history of the Commonwealth of Kentucky that such an honor had been accorded the body of a black. Hundreds of people, black and white, streamed into the auditorium and walked past the black casket, which contained the remains of the man who threw off the shackles of slavery and escaped to Ohio fifty-six years before. Lewis's long gray beard was combed into a close roll, and he presented an appearance of a well-earned rest. Many blacks were moved to tears while gazing on Clarke's well-chiseled face. Among the white men who paused by the casket were individuals of all professions.

At two o'clock Sunday afternoon, the body was removed from the auditorium to the church, where the funeral services took place. The funeral began with the reading of a scripture lesson and the singing of the song "Asleep in Jesus" by the choir. The Reverend Alex J. Chambers of Danville, Kentucky, read a sketch of Clarke's life, which included words of gratitude for the assistance given to Clarke during his last days by Charles Umbers of New Zealand. Reverend Chambers also mentioned newspapermen M. L. McClure and D. T. Baxter, whose dispatches were sent throughout the world describing the difficulties Clarke encountered in the latter stages of his life. Reverend Chambers called attention to the people of Kentucky who had allowed Lewis George Clark to starve or go to the poorhouse; when God raised up a friend in faraway New Zealand who sent him "succor" and saved him from the fate he dreaded, loud amens of the congregation could be heard on all sides. He mentioned that Harriet Beecher Stowe's daughter said Clarke was a fraud and tried to keep him from receiving benefits from the notoriety. Reverend Chambers also admonished Clarke. He declared "Lewis Clarke was both a success as well as a failure, just as Frederick Douglass was. He arose above the millions of his fellow slaves and sought liberty on the free soil of Canada. But his son here tells me that he deserted his own children, leaving them to shift for themselves, while he trotted around the world to be gaped at and admired as the original George Harris in Harriet Beecher Stowe's *Uncle Tom's Cabin*."[235]

Lewis Clarke's two daughters, Lettie Clarke Baker from Washington, DC, and Minnie Clarke Davis from Indianapolis, sent telegrams. Although they were unable to attend the funeral, each sent flowers, which were placed on the casket. Clarke's youngest son, James, read of Clarke's death while in Cleveland and immediately came by train to Lexington. He was studying law at Western Reserve University at the time. At the request of James, the remains of his father were shipped to Oberlin, Ohio, for interment at the side of Lewis's wife Emiline's grave.[236]

Major newspapers throughout the nation, such as the *Chicago Record,* the *Chicago Times Herald,* the *Washington Post,* the *Lexington Daily Leader,* the *Kansas City Journal,* the *San Francisco Call,* the Washington, DC, *Times,* and the *New York Sun* publicized full-page articles of Clarke's funeral. The Lexington, Kentucky, reporter D. T. Baxter, who was the primary United States contact with Charles Umber of Dunedin, New Zealand, sent Umber an article regarding Clarke's death. Baxter advised that he sent similar dispatches to all the leading newspapers in the United States. Although Clarke was never able to complete the writing of his life's story, what D. T. Baxter did was the next best thing. By way of his dispatches in December 1897, the entire world knew of Clarke's heroic contributions during a pivotal time in United States history.[237]

As more information became available, recent generations of the Lewis Clarke family had greater appreciation for what the patriarch accomplished in life. He is a model to his descendants as a man of principle, perseverance, and dedication. The family can always point to him with pride as an authentic American hero. Clarke's commitment to the antislavery movement and the civil rights of blacks frayed the fabric of his family structure, but his actions benefitted and changed a nation. He also made every effort to ensure that all knew of his affinity with the South. He was not embarrassed in the least by his experiences as a slave. He felt that he was the equal to any man and never considered himself as property. He said his former masters "could never claim *property* where they never had any." In 1845, such words by a black were considered those of an "uppity nigger" by most whites in America. Clarke in his inimitable way was succinctly uttering what is a fundamental premise within the Declaration of Independence: "We hold these truths to be self-evident: that all men are created equal; that they are endowed by their Creator with certain *unalienable* rights ; that among these are life, liberty, and the pursuit of happiness." Lewis's father, Daniel Clarke, and his compatriot minutemen who fought at Lexington, Concord, and Bunker Hill were among those who gave Thomas Jefferson the resolve and inspiration to write the Declaration. To Lewis and his father, the document was more than a compilation of ideals and concepts. They lived and acted upon its words.

Lewis wanted the white population of the entire nation to be aware of the atrocities that he and other Negroes suffered as a result of the evil institution. He was driven to ensure that the public clearly understood its repugnance and that it was contrary to fundamental Christian, American, and human values. He was proud of having escaped from slavery and brought others out of Southern states into the North and beyond to Canada. He told his story to all who would listen, most notably to Harriet Beecher Stowe, the author of *Uncle Tom's Cabin*. He proclaimed emphatically and consistently for over forty-five years that his numerous conversations with Mrs. Stowe were used as the basis for her political masterpiece. Almost to his dying day, he traveled the nation, telling riveting and witty revelations about his role as a conductor for the Underground Railroad. Lewis enjoyed the notoriety and celebrity he gained from his lectures and presentations. As a result of his life's journey, he became a bona fide American patriot. Regrettably, the annals of American history do not reflect in an appreciable way his role in bringing down America's most insidious experiment, the remnants of which impact negatively on African Americans to this day.

Chapter 8

A Family Victimized By The
Villainy Of The Times

At the time of Lewis's death, all his living children were over the age of twenty-five. At least four, Matte, Minnie, Cyrus, and Violetta (Lettie), had gone to Oberlin College and held respectable jobs as government employees or educators. James, the youngest, was attending law school at Western Reserve University in Cleveland when Lewis died. Why James was the only child of Lewis to attend his funeral remains a mystery, although one, Minnie, claimed she was ill when Lewis died. It is likely that the time Lewis spent away from his children caused some of them not to attend the funeral. Perusing articles of interviews published after Lewis came back to the United States, he repeatedly made statements in reference to the importance of educating his children. An example is how he responded to a *Washington Post* reporter's question: "How have you passed the time since you became a free man?"

"I was in Canada about nineteen years under the fugitive slave law. I owned a farm there, and worked it, but later sold it and used the money toward educating my children. I bought it about 1854, but did not go upon it until 1860. From there I went with my family to Oberlin, Ohio, to educate them."[238]

Was Lewis prevaricating about his concern about the children? There were different perspectives within the family. Minnie Clarke Davis, Clarke's second daughter, did not have misgivings about speaking glowingly about her father when she was interviewed in Indianapolis in 1891. She fondly reminisced about the times she spent with her father in East Sandwich, Canada, as a young child. Minnie described the relationship between Lewis and Mrs. Stowe as cordial and friendly over many years until "it was revealed a few months ago that the great authoress had a sad mental breakdown. Never a twelfth month was allowed to pass that Mrs. Stowe did not in some way emphasize her remembrance of the old man, whose related experience had turned to such good account in other days."[239] Minnie was married at the time of the interview to an eloquent young pastor, James Davis of the Allen Chapel African American Episcopal Church in Indianapolis. Minnie's younger sister was Violetta (Lettie) Clarke, who, in 1893, worked as a clerk in the Pension Department in Washington, DC. That same year, she married Henry E. Baker, a well-known patent attorney in the nation's capital.[240] Interestingly, Violetta and Henry married in Lexington, Kentucky, at the time Lewis was residing there. They went back to their home in Washington, DC, after the wedding. Clearly, Lewis gave away his daughter in marriage at the wedding. Obviously, having the wedding in Lexington was decided out of respect for Lewis. Surprisingly, no letters, articles, or ephemera are available elaborating on the marriage of two highly profiled members of the black intelligentsia of Washington, DC, not to mention the famous Lewis Clarke being the father of the bride.

The examples of cordial relationships Lewis had with his daughters before his death, did not portend the drastic changes that would take place within the family over the next decade. A variety of factors came into play. Certainly, one issue was the 1895 exposure of Lewis's abject poverty and the accompanying controversy with Harriet Beecher Stowe. These issues may have become embarrassing on several levels to the proud, relatively well-off siblings as well as other family members.

Although they marched to different drumbeats on the racial identity issue, Lewis's closest family member was his brother Milton. They went through many trials and triumphs together during the 1840s and '50s at the height of the antislavery movement. With encouragement from leaders of the abolitionist movement, the brothers moved from Oberlin to Massachusetts in the early 1840s. Milton remained in Cambridgeport (Cambridge) for the rest of his life. After their arrival, they were assisted by Aaron Safford, Harriet Beecher Stowe's brother-in-law. At the invitation of Aaron, Lewis lived at the Safford home for several years, and he also helped Milton find work in the Cambridge area as a caterer and waiter. When the Civil War began, Milton enlisted in the Twenty-Fourth Massachusetts Regiment at the age of forty-three, returning to the Boston area after the war ended. In 1870, Safford, a member of the Cambridge Common Council, arranged for Milton to replace him on the council. Clarke served out Aaron's term and was elected to a second term in 1872, becoming the first black elected member of the council in the city's history. Soon after his election, he resigned to take a job as a bank messenger for the US Sub Treasury in Boston, transporting millions of dollars of government money. He held that position for over twenty years. Milton remained a popular speaker in the Boston area and continued to highlight the importance of racial uplift before state legislators, conventions, and conferences as well as clubs and social gatherings.[241]

In 1895, Milton, responding to news reports of Lewis's dire financial and health circumstances, said he supported Lewis financially, on occasion, in his later years. He added, "I do not know how he got into his current financial circumstance. I have repeatedly helped Lewis and have got to the point where I cannot do anything more for him in Kentucky. I have sent a small sum just recently. What I do not understand is that his children don't do anything for him. He has several children down that way [Lexington]. I don't see why they do not all together help their father . . . Lewis and I have stuck together in times past. I shall not desert him now . . . The colored people down that way are under great obligation to Lewis. How he has worked for them! He has got them pensions, he has devoted his life to them and has made himself poor and out of recognition of his services to them they should do something for him."[242] When Lewis's died in 1897, Milton did not agree with Reverend Alexander Chamberlin's funeral sermon in Lexington about Lewis's role as a father nor the pastor's comments about his financial state. Contacted by the press after the funeral, Milton said defensively, "My brother did not die in destitute circumstances. As the morning papers stated, he received $350 [from Mr. Umbers] about a year ago, and it enabled him to live fairly comfortably until his death, and now there is enough to bury him. He owned a house and a piece of land in Kentucky, but was an old man and needed care. His children, of whom there are seven or eight, would not look out for him. He used up all the money he had bringing them up respectably, educating them, etc. but after he got too old to be of further use to them his children shipped [*sic*] him. I advised him to look after himself and let the children grow up as best they could, but he wouldn't do it. I am in my 78th year myself, but am still a young man and able to support myself and family. My brother and myself were born slaves in Kentucky, but I have lived here in Boston since I was 42 years old and consider this my home. When my brother has visited me here I have always urged him to come and live with me. I have sent him letters on the subject, but he persisted in remaining in the South."[243]

Among family members, John Milton Clarke clearly was Lewis's primary advocate. He was the only family member who challenged Harriet Beecher Stowe's inference that Lewis was a fraud and confirmed the facts of Lewis's *Narrative,* as well as Stowe's own, published statements that he was the prototype of George Harris of her novel. He also contended that *Uncle Tom's Cabin* would not have been written if he and his brother were not born because it was the story of their own lives. Milton, ironically, may have influenced other family members not to speak about the experiences he and Lewis had as Slaves. In essence, Milton's family quarrels, which became public, may have diminished the achievements of Lewis.

Jim Crow discriminatory laws in the South in the late 1900s, along with the infamous *Plessey v. Ferguson* "separate but equal" US Supreme Court decision in 1896, reflected a white backlash against blacks across the nation. Some can empathize with individuals and families who appeared to be white but with black blood in their veins, opting to cross over the white world to avoid rampant discrimination. Such was the case regarding Milton. He did not want publicity about the published *Narratives* concerning him and his brother Lewis to reemerge because the black blood issue would "embarrass his children and relatives."

Daniel A. Murray, a respected black historian of the day, served as assistant librarian at the United States Library of Congress. He held the position for over forty years. Murray was well-known for his writings on African American history, including his monumental manuscript *Historical and Biographical Encyclopedia of the Colored Race.* His connection with Milton began around 1899 and related to an assignment Murray was given by the Librarian of Congress, Herbert Putman. Murray was instructed "to secure a copy of every book and pamphlet in existence, by a Negro author, to be used in connection with the Exhibit of Negro Authorship at the Paris World's Fair of 1900 and later placed in the Library of Congress." From a list of 1,100 works, five hundred of these were to be displayed in Paris. A broader Exhibit of American Negroes was headed by NAACP founder W. E. B. Du Bois and included, beyond Murray's works, collections of art, photographs of homes, schools, and churches, and general life of Negroes in America.

One of the books Murray attempted to include in his exhibit was the 1846 *Narratives of the Sufferings of Lewis and Milton Clarke*. Murray sought to get a copy of the book from Milton, although he acknowledged that one copy was already in the Library of Congress. Nevertheless, he inserted a notice in the *Boston Transcript* newspaper inquiring whether Milton was still living, and if so, where? Murray received several letters back stating that Milton was living in Cambridge, Massachusetts. Murray sent letters to him asking for a copy of his book and received no reply. Murray then contacted his son who was a student at Harvard College and asked him talk to Milton about utilizing the book and to inquire about Milton's life after 1846. Murray's son reached Milton but felt coldly treated. Murray told his son to persist in his efforts, to no avail. Soon after the attempted contacts by Murray's son, on November 27, 1900, Milton sent by constable to all Boston newspapers the following court document:

> Know all men by these presents that I, J. Milton Clarke, of Cambridge, in the county of Middlesex and Commonwealth of Massachusetts, late messenger in the United States sub-treasury at Boston, fearing that certain matters, stories and so-called anecdotes, supposed to be connected with the early history of my life, may be published after my death, and there-by cause annoyance and embarrassment to my children and relatives, do hereby prohibit the printing and publishing of any such stories, so-called anecdotes, or anything relating to my life, except such facts as may be given out by my family after my death.
>
> This done in justice to my relatives and family, because such stories and anecdotes are overdrawn and misleading.

In witness whereof I have here unto set my hand and seal

J. Milton Clarke

Witnesses:

Margret Leamy

Isabel Clarke [granddaughter]

Middlesex, ss

Cambridge, Nov. 27, 1900

Then personally appeared the above named J. Milton Clarke and made oath that the above is his free act and deed.

Before me, Merman Bird

Justice of the Peace[244]

Although the initial press release was sent to Boston newspapers, Milton's story subsequently appeared in papers throughout the country. Daniel Murray believed that his attempts to reach Clarke led to Milton's court decree and its publication in the newspapers. As a result, Murray felt that he had to write a letter to the file of the Library of Congress fearful of possible legal action against him by Milton. Toward the end of Murray's letter, he went on a tirade, belittling Milton and questioning his veracity regarding his story as a slave as well as his purported connection with Harriet Beecher Stowe.[245] Clearly, Murray's professional pride was hurt immensely by Clarke's rejection. Murray was described as "being a great librarian and historian" as well as a "pioneer in the black history movement." He was fluent in several languages and testified before Congress against numerous segregation laws that were proposed during the years he was employed by the Library of Congress. Additionally, he was a colleague of W. E. B. Dubois among other members of the black elite of Washington, DC. Murray could not have taken lightly being rebuffed by a former slave with little if any formal education who was ashamed of his black heritage. In retaliation, it is likely that he did not promote the importance of the Clarke brothers to other historians as a result of his experience with Milton. That point was made clear in the above referenced letter of Murray's.

Washington, DC, at the turn of the nineteenth century, was arguably the African American intellectual capital of America, with the hub being Howard University. A negative word from Murray to that network certainly would not help sustain the historical significance of Lewis nor his brother beyond the turn of the century. Coincidentally, Milton Clarke's niece and Lewis Clarke's daughter Violetta Clarke Baker was working in the Library of Congress in Washington, DC, from approximately 1900 through 1923 as a high-level clerk. During Murray's attempts to contact her uncle Milton, was she working with the librarian? If so Milton's rejection had to be especially embarrassing to Violetta and her husband.[246] Since few blacks were working at the Library of Congress in those early days, one could surmise that Murray and Violetta knew each other well. Additionally Henry Baker, Violetta's husband, one of the most influential patent law practitioners in Washington, DC, at the time was working with W. E. B. DuBois on the Paris World's Fair of 1900 for Baker's exhibit on black inventors. He obviously was a colleague of Murray's when the conflict erupted concerning his wife's uncle, Milton Clarke.

There was no known response within the broader Clarke family in reaction to Milton's court order. The silence was deafening. When Milton's legal decree and article appeared in newspapers nationwide, it certainly had reverberations throughout the Clarke family. Was there an unwritten oath of silence made by the immediate descendants of Lewis and Milton in deference to Milton's wishes? If so, did that explain why subsequent generations of Clarkes did not know about Milton's decree as well as the significant contributions of Lewis? Were the family members embarrassed by the criticisms of Murray as to the truthfulness of the brothers' assertions concerning the writing of *Uncle Tom's Cabin* and therefore reluctant to talk about their lives? Answers to these questions can only be speculative. Added to the mystery is the fact that this author's mother, Virginia Clark, lived with her Aunt Violetta and Uncle Henry while she attended Howard University from 1920 to 1923, but evidently her aunt and uncle never mentioned anything about her grandfather Lewis, her granduncle Milton, or Murray. Virginia was also employed at the Library of Congress as an intern with Violetta while attending Howard and likely met Murray, who did not retire from the Library until 1923. Since Virginia was only in her late teens when she began living with the Bakers, they may have felt she was too young to handle the complicated family intrigues.

The "embarrassment" Milton identified in his decree was that he had black blood in his veins. Interviews over the years reflect Milton's consistent story that he was a "white slave" and that he did not consider himself to be black. His statements on the subject would vary from stating that "there is not one drop of Negro blood in me, so far as I can ascertain" to "somewhere a link was lost [in his lineage] and a single drop of dark blood flows in my veins, but it is not discernible."[247] Like Lewis, Milton did not have prototype black features. Milton married Abbey, who according to federal census records, was white. Milton, on the other hand, was alternately listed as "black/white" or "white" in such records. Newspaper accounts indicated that Milton's children unquestionably considered themselves white. Milton's legal decree, although directed toward those outside of the Clarke family, certainly made all members of the family, including those related to Lewis, think twice before disregarding the document, despite the difficulty of enforcing the order. The decree had to influence generations of Clarkes, not to promote the colorful and important history of either of the Clarke brothers. In contrast to Milton, Lewis did not agree with his brother on this matter. Milton's stand was contrary to Lewis's values and character. Lewis repeatedly pointed out, "Since I took my freedom I used my complexion as a means to an end. With this complexion I have never disowned my race. I say this with pride."[248]

Milton died on February 24, 1901, in Cambridge. However, even in death, he did not avoid controversy. The flowers were still fresh on his grave when Milton's two sons, Theodore P. B. and Eugene Clarke, contested Milton's will in court. Milton left $5 each to his sons. The bulk of the estate went to the widow of his son Cyrus, Isabella Clarke, and her daughter, also named Isabella. Both Isabellas had cared for Milton during his old age. As the hearing commenced, a key witness for Isabella Clarke and her daughter was Mrs. Fonseca, a sister of Mrs. Clarke, who told the court of a visit she made to the old man at which time she asked him if he had read in the newspapers about a colored man down South who was burned to death by vigilantes because of a crime he committed. She said, "Eugene Clarke was present. He spoke up and said something to the effect that he'd like to see all niggers tied to the floor and thrashed." Mrs. Fonseca went on to say said this hurt the old gentleman's feelings and he grew angry and said, "How can you say that, Gene, when you know how I was used down South. You have no respect for your father."

During the younger Isabella's testimony, she said on one occasion Gene Clarke had come to the house and remarked to his father, "You have no right to make a will without notifying me." Milton retorted, "I will not have you visiting this house if you can't act like a gentleman." This unfortunate exchange between father and son took place in the middle of January 1901, one month before Milton died. As the accusations between the brothers, Mrs. Clarke, and the eighteen-year-old daughter, became more heated, both Isabellas were reduced to tears. At one point Mrs. Clarke fainted.[249]

The brothers lost the case; however, two months later they filed an appeal, claiming that Milton was insane when he signed the will. No evidence was provided supporting their claim. Also, no record was found as to the results of the appeal.

An irony of the court case filed by the sons of Milton had the effect of doing exactly what Milton tried to avoid through his court decree the year before he died. Milton wanted to keep his family matters out of the media. Newspapers throughout the country covered the sordid details of his family's bickering, highlighting their black roots. The most shocking statement being the self-hate demonstrated by his son who said he would like all "niggers tied to the floor and thrashed."

From 1895 until Milton's death in 1901, a long series of earthshaking, very sensitive events concerning the Clarke brothers were on the world stage. This may explain why family members, for most of the twentieth century, were in the dark about the lives of Lewis Clarke as well as his younger brother Milton. The international controversy between Lewis the poor ex-slave and Harriet Beecher Stowe the world-renowned author was a no-win match up for Clarke. Likely, some family members may have sided with Stowe. The national exposure of Lewis's poverty was a slap in the face to the more affluent and proud children of Lewis as well as Milton. News coverage insinuated that the siblings were selfish.

If that were not enough, Milton added fuel to the flames with his court decree to stop people from inquiring about his past as a slave. The order was directed at an influential member of the black intelligentsia, Daniel Murray. Included in that elite group was Lewis's son-in-law, the iconic Henry Baker. Baker was married to Lewis's daughter Violetta (Lettie). Both Lettie and Henry worked closely with Murray. The coup de grâce is the pitiful court proceeding revealing the outrageous racist comment against blacks attributed to Milton's son. The entire aforementioned are covered by the national press and, in some cases, internationally. There is no wonder why many members of the Clarke family, particularly those who were living through the events described, did not talk in detail about their history. Shame, fear, and embarrassment kept them quiet. If any solace is to be derived from the events described is that they took place through no fault of Lewis Clarke.

Milton never embraced his black heritage. He considered the "one drop of black blood making one black" designation irrational. He was right. He wanted to protect his family from the vestiges of a racist society, attempting to hide black bloodlines; but the result of doing so was he died a broken man, leaving a family divided by race. Consider the bitter irony of a man who was an important figure in the antislavery movement who fought with the Union Army to free the slaves, knowing that his two sons hated blacks. All that transpired within Milton's family would have truly saddened Lewis.

Milton's efforts to cover up revelations of his life as a slave kept descendants on his side of the family in the dark about his black roots for over one hundred years. Through a genealogy web site, a woman contacted this author two years ago using a code name, and revealed that we are related. Specifically, she said she discovered that her husband is the great-greatgrandson of John Milton Clarke and the great-grandson of Theodore Parker B. Clarke, Milton's son. She said that her family, which is "white," had no knowledge of John Milton Clarke until her research traced her husband's lineage to my family tree. Her husband's family had assumed they were white. The revelations made them "slightly surprised." The author is continuing his correspondence with his cousins hoping that our families can, after all the lost years, celebrate together the accomplishments of two brave American heroes who happened to be brothers.

Lewis Clarke delivered his first speech in the Northeast in Brooklyn, New York, in 1842 before a crowd of thousands. He told of his experiences as a slave. Within his speech, he raised a historic question that is fundamental to race relations in this nation. "My grandmother was her master's daughter, and my mother was her master's daughter, and I was my master's son; so you see I han't got but one-eighth of the blood. Now admitting its right to make a slave of a full black nigger, I want to ask gentlemen acquainted with business, whether because I owe a shilling, I ought to pay a dollar?" Lewis was explaining that the "one drop of black blood makes you black" rule of white America not only defies logic but is fundamentally evil in its intent to stigmatize. Clarke, however, went on to make clear that he did not run away from being considered black but embraced the designation. Lewis was at the forefront of defining the African American race of today. The evil produced a good. African Americans can look very different from each other but bond together through customs, culture, community, and disposition. The one-drop rule united a group of people to fight the residual effects of slavery, i.e., segregation, racism, and injustice. Indeed, Lewis Clarke celebrated his black heritage.

Epilogue

From my teenage years through the age of thirty-three, conversations with my mother, Virginia Clark Gayton, about Lewis Clarke added few insights about him beyond what Harriet Beecher Stowe wrote in *The Key to Uncle Tom's Cabin*. My image of Lewis began to change in significant ways by way of a letter sent to my mother by her cousin Raymond Davis in February 1973. Davis, who lived in Columbus, Ohio, was the son of Minnie Clarke Davis, one of Lewis' daughters. Minnie was a favorite aunt of my mother and maintained contact with her by mail, while Virginia attended Howard University in Washington, DC, in the 1920s and years afterward. Aunt Minnie passed away in 1948 in Columbus, Ohio. Raymond and my mother never met until after my mother received Raymond's letter.

How my mother found out about Davis is a fascinating story. Mr. Davis was very active in his local African Methodist Episcopal (AME) Church in Columbus and served as a trustee in that church for many years. Because of Raymond's leadership role, he attended regional and national conferences on an annual basis. At the conferences, on numerous occasions, he would come in contact with Dr. Lee Terry, a surgeon, and his wife, Leota. Dr. Terry was also a longtime official in his AME Church in Reading, Pennsylvania. Over the years, Terry and Davis talked often during the times they attended the conferences.

Soon after a regional meeting of the church in the fall of 1972, my mother was visiting the Terrys at their home in Reading on her way to a national conference of the social action-focused Delta Sigma Theta Sorority. My father, John J. Gayton, had died three years earlier. Dr. Terry's connection with my mother went back to the days when both were undergraduates at Howard University in the 1920s. They were engaged for a short time, but my mother had to break the engagement and leave Howard because her father, Cyrus Clarke, Lewis Clarke's son, became very ill and she had to care for him in Vancouver, British Columbia, where her family resided.

Dr. Terry, his wife and my mother maintained contact, primarily through letters, for over fifty years. During the conversation she had with the Terrys in the fall of 1972, the topic included discussion of my mother's relative Minnie Clarke Davis and her son Raymond. Terry likely met Minnie while Virginia attended Howard. Minnie was teaching nearby in Bordentown, New Jersey, at the time. Discussion of Minnie obviously led to Dr. Terry saying that he knew a Raymond Davis from Columbus through the AME conferences they attended. My mother and Dr. Terry connected the dots, resulting in Dr. Terry sending Davis a note asking him if his mother was Minnie Clarke Davis, and if so, his good friend Virginia was his mother's, Minnie's, niece living in Seattle.

With the relationship verified, the very elated Davis sent Dr. Terry a long letter on December 27, 1972, which provided a plethora of information about the mutual relatives of Davis and his newly located cousin Virginia. Davis exclaimed, "Isn't it singular that Velma [his deceased wife] and I have enjoyed your hospitality on several occasions, and talked, and talked about everything, and never once did the conversations turn to Seattle and Vancouver, where any chance remark that I once had an Uncle [Cyrus Clark] out on the coast or you Doc, could have mentioned about Virginia Clark being in Howard at the same time, and this would have started a whole chain of relationships between us 'Davis's' and Clarks.' Oh how thankful I am to learn of cousin Virginia! Please send me Virginia Gayton's address at your earliest convenience!"

Ray Davis sent my mother a letter dated February 9, 1973:

> My dear cousin Virginia. You cannot imagine how overjoyed I am at this moment. I just received your airmail letter a few moments ago and I am sitting down to answer it right away. I have so many things crowding into my mind that I want to tell you. I know that I won't (sic) be able think of all that I want to bring you up to date on concerning our distinguished ancestor [Lewis Clarke].

Within the letter he went on to provide information about his family, with special emphasis on his mother, Minnie Clark Davis. Clearly, my mother already knew a great deal about Minnie through the letters she sent my mother as well as the likelihood that she visited her often while she was a student at Howard University. Raymond also mentioned in his letter that Aunt Minnie was one of the first persons of color to graduate from Oberlin College in Ohio.

With regard to Lewis, Davis wrote that in December of 1897 his mother got word from Cyrus Clark (Minnie's brother and my mother's father) that Lewis had died. Minnie was ill and in bed at the time with "either typhoid or malaria fever, and could not attend the funeral." One in the family sent Minnie a copy of a four-column spread in the daily newspaper the *Lexington Leader* dated December 19, 1897. Raymond was nine years old at the time of Lewis's passing. Davis went on to say in his letter that he did not recall his mother talking much about Lewis other than he was "a great talker and a wanderer. She may have told us more about him but I do not recall, hearing her do so." Davis recalled that Minnie kept the newspaper article about Clarke's death in a trunk. When Minnie died in 1948, one of Davis' nieces had all the personal effects of his mother including the newspaper article. Davis wrote that it was not until 1966 that he began to wonder about the article as well as a book that Clarke and his brother Milton had dictated to a Reverend Joseph Lovejoy in 1846. It was entitled *Narratives of the Sufferings of Lewis and Milton Clarke, Sons of a Soldier of the Revolution During a Captivity of More Than Twenty Years among the Slaveholders of Kentucky (One of the So-Called Christian States of North America) Dictated by Themselves, 1846.* Davis, evidently, was not aware of the book dictated by Lewis Clarke to Reverend Lovejoy and published in 1845, entitled *Narrative of the Sufferings of Lewis Clarke: During a Captivity of More Than Twenty-Five Years among the Algerines of Kentucky, One of the So-Called Christian States of North America, Dictated by Himself.* Davis also pointed out to my mother that he had a portrait photograph of Lewis taken a few years before his death.

Davis also informed her that after much research he had located Lewis's grave site in Oberlin, Ohio. Managers of the Westward Cemetery initially indicated that the grave could not be located. Further investigation revealed that the grave marker was covered by grass and not easily seen by the naked eye. Davis purchased a new, much larger marker and had inscribed "Lewis Clarke, March 1815-December 1897, The Original George Harris of Harriet Beecher Stowe's Uncle Tom's Cabin."

The information Raymond Davis provided about the *Narratives* of the Clarke brothers and the full-page Lexington, Kentucky, story of Lewis's death in the city's press, as well as the location of his grave site, were all new revelations to my mother and our immediate family. Mr. Davis boarded a plane to Seattle on September 4, 1974. After his arrival, thirty-four members of my family, including aunts, uncles, in-laws, cousins, brothers, and sisters as well as my mother's sister Ruth and her son John, met at my mother's house to welcome Raymond. The family gathering was a joyous occasion. All of my family was impressed with Raymond's wit and outgoing personality. We were especially appreciative of the new information he provided about Lewis Clarke.

Two weeks later, after arriving home in Columbus, Davis set a letter to all who attended his welcome in Seattle:

> I don't know how to begin this letter of—THANKS— to each one of you whom I had the delightful pleasure of meeting for the first time on Wednesday, September 4th at the home of my cousin, Mrs. Virginia Gayton. Any way, you have no idea how thrilled I was to meet you for the first time. . . . It was an experience that I shall *never* forget.

Raymond Davis died in 1984 in Columbus, Ohio. No information is available concerning ongoing communication between my mother and Raymond beyond the abovementioned letters he sent. However, his visit, along with the knowledge that Lewis Clarke and his brother had dictated a book of their early years as slaves, changed in a profound way our family's impression of Lewis. Up to that point in time, we did not realize that his story extended beyond the inner circle of interesting family conversation. Lewis certainly was more famous than all of Clarke's descendants in Seattle realized. After somewhat minimal investigation, we were made aware that the narratives of Lewis and Milton had been republished by the Arno Press and the *New York Times* in 1969 under the broad title of *The Anti-Slavery Crusade in America*. I, including several members of my family, purchased the Clarke brothers' book. The stories of their enslavement and the atrocities they suffered and witnessed were abominable. Reading the *Narratives* still brings tears to my eyes.

I considered the *Narratives* of such importance I purchased an extra copy to give to one of my favorite undergraduate professors at the University of Washington, Dr. Thomas Pressly. Dr. Pressly was a full professor in the history department, with his area of concentration being the antebellum South and the Civil War. He was deservedly identified by student polls as one on the most inspiring lecturers on campus and was highly respected by his colleagues for his research and publications. Dr. Pressly had the unique capability of bringing history to life, especially through the journals, diaries, and letters of relevant figures of the times.

After I bought the book for the professor, I wrote a short note on its inside page expressing the pride I had in Clarke and that I wanted Dr. Pressly in particular to have a copy because of how he inspired me over the years. I telephoned the professor and said I would like to meet with him, but I did not mention the *Narrative*. He invited me the university's faculty club for lunch. Toward the end of the meal, I told him that I had a gift of appreciation for him, and I gave him the book. He glanced at my note on the inside of the book and was expressionless. I was shocked and disappointed by his response. He said, in essence, that slave narratives were in abundance in the middle 1800s and were not regarded as having much historical relevance. A primary concern of historians' familiar with that period of United States history, according to Dr. Pressly, was that the slaves dictated their stories to abolitionists who were zealots on behalf of the abolitionist cause and invariably exaggerated the recollections of the slaves. After the lunch, I was embarrassed that I had given him the book. He never gave it back, but my clear impression was that he did not want the book. As a true Southern gentleman, I felt that he kept it out of courtesy. As the result of Dr. Pressley's observations, the elation that I had about Clarke after Cousin Raymond Davis's visit to Seattle was wiped away. Based upon what Dr. Pressly said, my image of Clarke reverted back to him being merely an interesting character within the context of our family history. For the next few years, whatever interest I had to do further research on Clarke was no longer a priority.

Subsequently, while teaching at Florida State University, I came in contact, while jogging, with a FSU history professor, Peter Ripley.

After several weeks of jogging and passing the time of day, I asked him what his area of specialty was in the history department. He told me that his research focus was on slavery in the United States and the abolitionist movement prior to the Civil War. I responded by saying that I had a personal interest in that period of history because my great-grandfather was a black abolitionist. I quickly added that I was sure he would not know anything about him because, at best, my great-grandfather probably was regarded as an insignificant figure within the abolitionist movement and he wouldn't know anything about him. Pete said, "Try me. What was his name?" I said, "Lewis Clarke." Excitedly, Pete said, "My God, I have all sorts of literature about him." He went on to say that he was member of a team of researchers working on *The Frederick Douglass Papers* project headed by Dr. John Blassingame at Yale University, and that his research clearly indicated that Lewis Clarke played an important role in the movement. He added that Clarke was especially active in Ontario, Canada, where large numbers of escaped slaves settled before the beginning of the Civil War. I was speechless. Here I was, over three thousand miles away from my home and serendipitously came in contact with a man who was probably one of only a handful of people in the world who would have an in-depth awareness of the life of my great-grandfather. Receiving this information from Pete in such a casual way added to the surreal nature of the revelation. Even without Pete telling me of his research, he would have become a friend of mine. Becoming close with someone within a short period of time was out of character for me. However, our common political outlook, sense of humor, and somewhat laid-back personalities made it fun to be around each other and made Pete an exception from the way I usually connected with people.

Pete provided me with reams of articles, manuscripts, and papers he had about Clarke, including information on the years after Clarke published his *Narrative* in 1845. Browsing through the material made me realize the Clarke was indeed a significant figure during the later stages of the abolitionist period and remained a well-known activist for human rights through the early 1890s. The misgivings that Dr. Thomas Pressly, my old college mentor at the University of Washington, had about Clarke were not accurate. I did not have any anger toward Dr. Pressly for his opinion, but I was obviously disappointed. Most academic historians of Dr. Pressly's generation had similar perspectives regarding the slave narratives. Dr. Ripley represented a younger and more enlightened cadre of researchers of the slavery period. Their positive perspective of the value of slave narratives was likely influenced by new, more precise research.

Due to my teaching and research obligations within the Department of Public Administration at FSU, I was unable to do the kind of in-depth evaluation of the treasure trove of papers that Pete gave me. Also, in reading many of the articles provided by Peter, I was unable to place them in context until I conducted additional research on my own years later. I told myself that I would take the time to thoroughly examine the material. My schedule and procrastination never led me in that direction while I resided in Tallahassee. Continuing the intended research on Lewis Clarke was put on hold for another twenty-five years.

My retirement from working in the public and private sectors, along with no immediate full-time job commitments, finally gave me the opportunity to begin outlining the direction I wanted to go regarding the life story of Lewis Clarke, not just his years reflected in his 1845 *Narrative*. My initial draft outline focused on an autobiography about me with considerable emphasis on my paternal grandfather John T. Gayton as well as Clarke. I considered them the patriarchs of the respective families. I began researching and writing with that format in mind. New research led me in a different direction. As I grew older, I realized that time was not on my side and that I had an obligation to be more committed to do justice to the memory of my ancestors, which meant finishing the manuscript I started writing. As I began to review the documents I had from my Florida State University colleague, as well as other new and revealing research concerning Lewis Clarke, I came to the realization that any autobiography about me or further focus on my paternal grandfather had to be placed on hold. The significant volume of documentation about Clarke justified greater visibility beyond family members. I concluded that Clarke's story was of national importance. Whether the nation would feel the same as I did would be another matter. Whatever the reaction, I felt that the story needed to be told.

Peter Ripley's material on Clarke's life, particularly after the publication of Lewis's 1845 *Narrative*, shed new light on his character as well as his achievements. His material triggered additional research in libraries as well as the Internet—especially newspaper articles about him. Information supplied by my daughter Cynthia Gayton, a lawyer in

Washington, DC, led to her doing extensive research in the US Library of Congress as well as the Internet. Clarke's personal reflections within the material also provided heretofore generally unknown revelations about his close "professional" relationship with Harriet Beecher Stowe as well as other major players in the abolitionist movement. Little known facts about his role in leading the Radical Abolitionist Party in Busti, Chautauqua County, New York, and Sugargrove, Warren County, Pennsylvania, as well as making a safe haven for escaped slaves in Amherst burg, Ontario, Canada, revealed a side of his past not reflected in his 1845 *Narrative*.

As I was delving into my writing, a public historian from the Sugar Grove, Pennsylvania, Historical Commission, was searching the Internet in July 2009 to find information about Lewis. The gentleman read a front-page article in the *Seattle Times* dated January 19, 2005, which reflected my relationship to Clarke.[250] The historian corresponded with me inquiring about my great-grandfather and wanted information for his research about Clarke's children, one of whom was my grandfather Cyrus H. Clark. I provided the information and indicated that I would contact him if I found out anything new. Another communication from the historian referred to an article in the *Washington Post* was dated May of 1890. The extensive coverage indicated that Clarke had been invited to come from Oberlin, Ohio, to speak at the Nineteenth Street Baptist Church in Washington, DC, about his ventures as well as his memories of Harriet Beecher Stowe.[251]

There was one statement Clarke made in the article that gave me the missionary zeal to complete Lewis's story. Clarke said he was in the process of getting a book out on his life and that after leaving Washington, D. C., he would be going to New York and Philadelphia to work out the details. He pointed out that he particularly wanted to correct some of the misleading information that Mrs. Stowe had in her book.

Extensive investigations have not discovered whether the book had actually been published. Not having the written story of his entire life, we the family and the public are less fortunate as a result. I hope that this publication about his exciting and significant contributions to American history help to some degree to fulfill my great-grandfather's wish.

Finally, the multiplier effect of the material I collected about Clarke made it imperative for me to concentrate all the time I could on this remarkable man whose accomplishments and experiences have been basically unknown to the general public for over a century.

Appendix

Summary Of Harriet Beecher Stowe's *Uncle Tom's Cabin*

Uncle Tom's Cabin is considered one of the most popular novels ever written. However, today's general public, although aware of the book, have scant knowledge of its major themes or its importance. Additionally large segments of the population perceive the book as racist and do not want to give it credence by affording it any in-depth analysis. Many have come to that conclusion without having read the original novel. Such perceptions of the story came primarily from the portrayal of the title character, Uncle Tom, within the plethora of dime museums and minstrel shows produced for more than fifty years after the publication of the book. Tom was seen as a shuffling, subservient, groveling fool in such productions, hence the pejorative term "Uncle Tom." Stowe had no legal authority over the shows nor did she approve of them. A close reading of the book portrays Tom as a heroic, nonviolent figure who sacrificed his life rather than reveal the whereabouts of two escaped female slaves to the evil master Simon Legree.

A summary of the novel is included with the appendix for two reasons: one, as indicated above, is to provide an accurate understanding of Mrs. Stowe's novel, and the other is to show interesting similarities of the broad themes and characters when comparing *Uncle Tom's Cabin* and the *Narrative of the Sufferings of Lewis Clarke*.

Harriet Beecher Stowe's classic story of *Uncle Tom's Cabin* begins on the Kentucky plantation of Mr. and Mrs. Selby and their child George, near the village of Paint Lick. The Selbys are good and kind individuals, especially in comparison to other slave owners. Uncle Tom is one of their slaves, and they have deep affection for him. However, Mr. Selby is in financial difficulty and is seeking a way to reduce his debt and save the plantation. The situation is so dire that he starts conversations with a slave trader. As a result, Mr. Selby makes an agreement with the trader to sell Tom and young Harry. Harry is the child of his servant Eliza, a quadroon woman, and a rebellious mulatto slave, George Harris (Lewis Clarke), from a nearby plantation. Harris has been hired out by his master to work in a bagging factory where he is held in high regard as a worker. He invents a machine for the cleaning of hemp, which requires the mechanical genius of an Eli Whitney.

George Harris is a handsome, manly person with a pleasing manner and a favorite among the factory workers. His appearance and fluent talk makes his master feel intimidated. George is viewed as too uppity by his master despite his skills as a weaver. He is subjected to extremely hard work away from the factory, with the intention of breaking his spirit. George has freedom to come and go as he pleases, because the factory manager trusts him.

As the result of matchmaking by Mrs. Selby, George and Eliza marry. Mrs. Selby was pleased to bring together George, her handsome favorite, with Eliza. George and Eliza see each other frequently for approximately two years. With the birth of their child, Harry, Eliza becomes content and happy until George is rudely torn from his kind employer and brought under the tight control of his legal owner. His former employer tries, but fails, to convince George's master to let him come back to the factory.

George explains to Eliza that he is escaping to Canada because of his problems with his master. Eliza attempts to convince George not to leave, but his mind is made up. Eliza exclaims, "After all he is your master." George responds, "My master! Who made him my master? What right has he to me? I am a better man than he is. I know more about business than he does, I am a better manager than he is . . . I've learned in spite of him, and now what right has he to make a drag horse of me?"[252] To Eliza's dismay, George tells her of his master plans to have him marry another woman, and if he does not accept, he will sell him down the river.

George tells Eliza that in view of the circumstances, he is going to Canada, and when he saves enough money, he will buy her and young Harry. He swears he will not be taken by the slave catchers. "I won't be taken, Eliza. I'll die first! I'll be free or I'll die!"[253] He bids Eliza a heartbreaking good-bye and leaves for Canada.

After George's departure, Eliza overhears the bargain Mr. Selby makes with the slave trader, Haley, about the sale of young Harry and the loyal Tom. Eliza tells Tom of the impending sale and her decision to flee the plantation with her son. In grief, Tom collapses in his chair; yet he understands her decision to leave, telling her that it is her right to leave. Although Tom's wife, Chloe, encourages him to also escape, Tom expresses his understanding of the dilemma facing Mr. Selby and the prospect of losing the plantation if the sale is not agreed upon. He does not want to break the trust of Mr. Selby. Tom says "it is better for me to go than break up the place and sell it all."[254]

With the escape of Eliza and Harry, Mrs. Selby has to confront the anger of Mr. Haley, the slave trader, and she promises him she will find Harry and Eliza. Mrs. Selby, however, is pleased with the escape. Tom prepares to leave with Haley and is soon on his way to join his new master, Mr. Augustine St. Clare, in Louisiana. Mrs. Selby promises Tom that she will buy him back as soon as she and her husband can accumulate enough money.

Haley and two of Selby's slaves begin to follow the runaway, Eliza. The slaves, who secretly approve of Eliza's escape, purposely lead Haley on a circuitous route toward the general direction of Eliza's escape route, giving her time to distance herself from her pursuers. Haley and the slaves soon catch up with her as she and Harry are going down the bank of the Ohio River.

Stowe describes the scene: "Right on behind they came, and nerved with strength such as God only gives only to the desperate, with one wild cry and flying leap, she vaulted sheer over the turbid current by the shore, on to the raft of ice beyond. . . the huge fragment of ice on which she alighted pitched and creaked as her weight came on it but staid [sic] there not a moment . . . she leaped to another and still another cake. Her shoes were gone, her stockings cut from her feet while blood marked her every step, but she saw nothing, felt nothing, till. . . she saw the Ohio side and a man helped her up the bank."[255]

Eliza and Harry are assisted for one evening by an Ohio senator and his wife, Mr. and Mrs. Bird. Eventually they take Eliza and the child to a Quaker village where they unite with her husband George Harris. The Quaker family of Rachel and Simeon Halliday accommodate them for one evening before continuing on the Underground Railroad, moving north.

St. Clare, a relatively benevolent master, has a young daughter, Evangeline (Eva), who shares Tom's deep religious faith. Eva has a disdain for the way slaves are treated. She and Tom have long conversations, and he comes to consider Eva as the embodiment of Christ. Eva grows deeply disturbed by the injustices of slavery. Her concern begins to affect her health and wears down her already fragile constitution, resulting in her eventual death. Shortly afterward her father passes away, and Tom is left in the hands of St. Clare's evil wife, Marie. She holds no empathy for the plight of the slaves on the plantation. Marie soon decides to move back to her parents' home and sell all the slaves.

Meanwhile in Kentucky, Tom's wife, Chloe, after learning of Tom's situation, begins hiring her services out in odd jobs in order to save money to purchase Tom and have him return to the Selby farm.

Augustine St. Clare's cousin from New England, Ophelia, has been living with the family. She is a somewhat austere, pious woman who supports the abolitionist cause. Although an abolitionist, she has preconceived, negative notions about slaves. Little Eva's influence on her makes her confront her biases, and she becomes more enlightened and understanding of the blacks on the plantation. This new awareness and empathy leads Ophelia to confront Marie in an attempt to convince her not to sell the slaves, particularly Tom. Augustine, before he died, promised Tom that he would not be sold. Nevertheless, Marie rebuffs both Ophelia and Augustine.

Tom, along with a pretty mulatto slave, Emmiline, is sold to Simon Legree, an evil plantation owner on the Red River [Red River Parish, Louisiana]. Legree is known to work his slaves exceptionally hard, leading to the deaths of many them. When Tom arrives at the rundown Legree plantation, he finds it guarded by ferocious dogs. He also comes across Legree's mean-spirited overseers, slaves Sambo and Quimbo.

Although Legree considers Tom to be an excellent worker, he begins to dislike and mistrust him when he notices that Tom is disturbed when he disciplines the other slaves, particularly when they have difficulty working in the hot cotton fields. From time to time, Tom would put cotton balls in the baskets of the women slaves to ensure that their baskets meet the weight requirements Legree demands. Overseer Sambo informs Legree of what Tom is doing to assist the women. Legree confronts Tom and threatens to "break him in." Legree then relents somewhat, realizing that the other slaves in the field respect Tom and acknowledge that he is a superb worker. Legree goes as far as far as telling Tom that he will make him an overseer if he keeps out of trouble. Tom refuses his offer because he cannot carry out the discipline against his fellow slaves. Legree becomes livid and yells, "You pretend to be so pious. . . didn't you see in your own bible that 'servants obey yer masters'? Ain't I yer master? . . . Ain't yer mine body and soul?"[256] Tom replies that he only belongs to Christ, not Legree nor any other man. At that point Legree orders Quimbo and Sambo to beat Tom. They comply and then drag him away.

Although racked with pain, Tom continues his acts of kindness toward the other slaves and helps them fill their cotton baskets. He has a vision of heaven one night, which gives him the encouragement he needs to continue on as he drifts off to sleep.

The assistance Tom gives to the slaves enrages Legree all the more. When the two slaves, Emmeline and Cassy, escape, Legree demands that Tom tell him all he knows. Tom admits that he knew of their plans to escape as well as their whereabouts; however, he refuses to give him any details. Legree reacts by beating him more severely than ever. Tom looks up to Legree and speaks, "Ye poor miserable critter. . . there ain't no more ye can do [to me]. I forgive ye with all my soul," and then he faints entirely away. Tom is not quite gone when the overseers Sambo and Quimbo approach him. Feeling remorseful, Quimbo says, "O, Tom, we's ben so wicked to ye." Tom, faintly replies, "I forgive ye with all my heart."[257]

Two days later, George Selby, the son of Mr. and Mrs. Selby, the first owners of Tom, arrives at the Legree plantation with the money Tom's wife, Chloe, had saved to buy back Tom and take him to the Selby home. It is too late. After a short tearful exchange between them, Tom passes away with a smile on his face.

Cassey and Emmeline are successful in eluding the slave catchers Legree sends after them. They are able to make their way to the nearby town with disguises—Cassey as a wealthy Creole woman and Emmeline as her servant. They board a ferry bound for the north. Young George Selby is also a passenger on the boat and befriends a passenger by the name of Madame de Thoux. George and Madame de Thoux discover an amazing coincidence through their conversation—she is the sister of George Harris. She asks what happened to her brother over the years and how he was doing. Young George tells her that Harris escaped to Canada with his wife and child, and then Madame de Thoux begins to cry. She explains that George and she were sold away from each other when they were children. Young George explains that George Harris married a very attractive servant of the Selbys named Eliza. Cassey overhears the conversation and asks young George if he knows the names of the people who bought Eliza from the Selbys. He replies that it is a family named Simmons, at which point Cassey faints. Hearing this confirms that Eliza is her long-lost daughter. Days later, young George sends Cassey the bill of sale which undoubtedly verified the truth of the story. Madame de Thoux and Cassey now have a common bond and travel to Canada in search of George Harris and Eliza and finally locate them in Montreal where they reveal their identities to them.

After an emotional reunion, Madame de Thoux explains to George and Eliza that her husband, a Frenchman, passed away leaving her with a small fortune, which she intends to divide among the family. George accepts his sister's generosity and moves to France with Eliza, where he earns a university degree.

Political troubles in France lead Harris and Eliza to move to Africa, where they remain. Harris's views about America and his future interests are expressed in a long letter to a friend. He starts off by saying he is not comfortable living in America, although he probably could get by; however, he simply has no desire to do so. He goes on to say, "My sympathies are not for my father's race, but for my mother's. To him I was no more than a fine dog or a horse. To my heart broken mother I was a child, and though I never saw her after the sale that separated us till she died, yet I know she always loved me dearly. I know it in my own heart. When I think of all she suffered, of my own early sufferings, of the distresses and struggles of my heroic wife, of my sister, sold in the New Orleans slave market—though I hope to have no unchristian sentiments, yet I may be excused for saying I have no wish to pass myself as an American [white] or to identify myself with them. It is with the oppressed, enslaved African race that I cast my lot; and, if I wished anything, I would wish myself two shades darker, rather than lighter."[258]

Young George Selby returns from Legree's farm and tells Chloe and the other servants of Tom's death. George returns Chloe's money she gave him from her earnings to free Tom. She, in turn, with trembling hands, gives the money to Mrs. Selby saying, "Don't never want to see hear on't again. Jist as I knew 'twould be, sold and murdered on demar' old plantations!"[259]

A month later, George Selby appears before a slave gathering on the plantation. Amid sobs, tears, and shouts, he reads and presents each slave with a certificate of freedom. He concludes, "Think of your freedom every time you see Uncle Tom's Cabin; and let it be a memorial to put you all in the mind to follow his steps, and be as honest and faithful and Christian, as he was."[260]

Timeline Report for Lewis G. Clarke

Yr/Age	Event	Date/Place
1500	World History Colonialism	Bet. 1500–1900 World
1500	World History Atlantic Slave Trade	Bet. 1500–1900 Africa, Europe, North America, South America, Caribbean
1750	World History The Industrial Revolution	Bet. 1750–1850 Great Britain
1800	US History Western Expansion	Bet. 1800–1900 USA
1810	Central America/Caribbean Mexican War of Independence	Bet. 1810–1821 Mexico
1815	Canadian History The Great Migration of Canada	Bet. 1815–1850 Canada
1815	Birth	Mar 1815 Madison County, Kentucky, USA
1821 5	Becomes the slave of John and Betsey Campbell Banton It was the custom of the day for a woman who married would be provided a young slave as part of her dowry. Lewis was selected.	1821 Madison County, Kentucky, USA
1821 5	Death Samuel Campbell, maternal grand-father of Lewis Clarke.	1821 Lexington, Kentucky, USA
1831 15	Residence Sold as a slave to General Thomas Kennedy.	1831 Garrard County, Kentucky, USA
1841 26	Departure Escapes from slavery, to connect with his brother Milton whom he believes is in Canada.	Aug 1841 Garrard County, Kentucky, USA
1842 26	Arrival Reconnects with brother Milton after determining he was not residing in Canada.	Jan 1842 Oberlin, Ohio, USA
1842 27	Departure Leaves Oberlin to rescue his brother Cyrus from slavery in Lexington, Kentucky.	Jul 1842 Oberlin, Ohio, USA
1842 27	Near Capture After rescuing brother Cyrus in Lexington, Lewis and brother Milton go on a speaking tour in Ohio and are nearly captured by slave-catchers from Kentucky.	01 Sep 1842 Madison, Lake, Ohio, USA
1842 27	Departure At the request of anti-slavery leaders	15 Sep 1842 Oberlin, Lorain County, Ohio, USA

in the Northeast, he departs for
Cambridgeport , Mass. to help support
the abolitionist movement.

1842 27	Residence Begins a seven year residence with Aaron Safford and wife Mary Safford, stepsister of Harriet Beecher Stowe.	30 Sep 1842 Cambridge City, Middlesex, Massachusetts
1842 27	Speech: "Leaves from a Slave's Journal of Life" Historical speech to thousands about his life as a slave.	20 Oct 1842 Brooklyn, Kings, New York, USA
1842 27	Begins Dictation of his Life Narrative Begins dictation of his life as a slave to Rev. Joseph C. Lovejoy.	Dec 1842 Cambridge City, Middlesex, Massachusetts
1844 28	Meets with Harriet Beecher Stowe Has first of many meetings with Mrs. Stowe, covering several years, at the home of her sister-in-law, Mary Safford.	Jan 1844 Cambridge City, Middlesex, Massachusetts
1845 29	Publication "Narrative of the Sufferings of Lewis Clarke During a Captivity of More Than Twenty-Five Years Among the Algerines of Kentucky, One of the So Called Christian States of North America." Placed in the U. S. Library of Congress.	1845 Boston, Suffolk, Massachusetts, USA
1846 30	Publication Narrative of the Sufferings of Lewis and Milton Clarke."	1846 Boston, Massachusetts
1847 31	Speech To a gathering of thousands at the Tremont Temple, he is the first fugitive slave to stand up in a public assembly to argue the question of slavery with a slave owner.	1847 Boston, Suffolk, Massachusetts, USA
1849 33	Departure Moves from Cambridge to Busti, to be the conductor of the underground railroad located in that village.	1849 Busti, Chautauqua, New York.
1849 33	Marriage Catherine Storum	25 Feb 1849 Busti, Chautauqua, New York.
1850 34	US History Fugitive Slave Law of 1850 passed by Congress. Fugitive slaves no longer safe in the Northern states. Slave owners could seek them out throughout the nation.	1850
1851 36	Destination "Call for North American Convention" ,Henry Bibb asks 71 Black leaders, including Clarke, to meet in Toronto to	Aug 1851 Toronto, Ontario, Canada

discuss the "emancipation of our race."

	1851 36	Encounter A close encounter with bounty hunters attempting to take him back to Kentucky. A chase ensues.	Oct 1851 Busti, Chautauqua, New York.
	1852 36	Publication Harriet Beecher Stowe's "Uncle Tom's Cabin" published.	1852 Boston, Suffolk, Massachusetts, USA
	1853 37	Departure Moves to Canada, but travels back and forth to assist fugitive slaves in Busti.	1853 Windsor, Essex, Ontario, Canada
	1853 37	Dinner Meeting At Harriet Beecher Stowe's invtation, Clarke has dinner with Mrs Stowe and her children. This was their last meeting together.	1853 Andover, Essex, Massachusetts, USA
	1853 37	Publication Harriet Beecher Stowe's "Key to Uncle Tom's Cabin" published.	1853 Boston, Suffolk, Massachusetts, USA
	1853 38	Convention Serves as Vice President of Continental League of Afro-American Race, which holds the North American Convention of Colored People. Josiah Henson is President.	16 Jun 1853 Amherstburg, Essex, Ontario, Canada
	1854 39	Keynote Speaker A keynote speaker at the first convention of the Republican Party.	06 Jul 1854 Jackson, Jackson, Michigan, USA
	1856 41	Radical Abolitionist Party Presides over Radical Abolitionist Party Convention, as the organization's President.	09 Aug 1856 Sugargrove, Pennsylvania
	1857 42	U.S. History U. S. Supreme Court, hands down its decision on the famous Dred Scott v. Sanford case, stipulating that slaves were not citizens and had no right to bring suit in the courts.	06 Mar 1857 United States
	1859 44	Meeting with John Brown Along with several other Black leaders, he meets with John Brown to discuss attack on Harpers Ferry.	Mar 1859 Detroit, Wayne, Michigan, USA
	1859 44	Speaker Featured speaker and Vice-President, "New England Colored Citizens Convention", at the Meionaon and Tremont Temple in Boston.	Aug 1859 Boston, Suffolk, Massachusetts, USA
	1859 44	Marriage Emiline Bell Walker	08 Dec 1859 Detroit, Wayne, Michigan, USA.

1874 58	Departure Sells farm property and moves family from Windsor to Oberlin, Ohio.	1874 Windsor, Essex, Ontario, Canada
1876 60	On Retainer On retainer by a group of prosperous planters in Kentucky to help build the Black labor force in that state. Travelled between Oberlin and Kentucky for many years.	1876 Oberlin, Ohio, USA
1876 61	Testimony Testified before U. S. Congress, Ways and Means Committee regarding economic plight of former slave refugees returning to the U. S.	May 1876 Washington D. C.
1880 64	Residence	1880 Oberlin, Lorain, Ohio, United States.
1891 76	Last Meeting After an extensive nation wide speaking tour, he has his last meeting with his brother Milton after a speaking engagement in Boston.	20 May 1891 Cambridge, Middlesex, Massachusetts, USA
1892 76	Residence In 1892 he moves to Lexington, Kentucky from Oberlin.	1892 Lexington, Kentucky, USA
1895 80	Destitute Economically destitute and physically feeble.	May 1895 Lexington, Kentucky, USA
1896 80	U. S. History The U. S. Supreme Court upholds segregation of the races in its "separtate but equal" doctrine set forth in Plessy v. Ferguson.	1896 USA
1896 81	U. S.History. Harriet Beecher Stowe (1811-1896) dies in Harford, Connecticut.	01 Jul 1896 Hartford, Hartford, Connecticut, USA
1897 82	Death He passed away in his sleep.	16 Dec 1897 Lexington, Kentucky, USA
1897 82	Burial	20 Dec 1897 Oberlin, Lorain County, Ohio, USA

Index

Acknowledgments

My deepest gratitude must be directed to my great-grandfather Lewis G. Clarke for giving me the inspiration to write about him. Throughout my life, I learned more insights, not just about his accomplishments but his character. However, it was not until the last decade that it became clear to me that his contributions to American history justified an audience far beyond his immediate family, thus the publication of this labor of love and respect.

My mother, Virginia Emily Clark Gayton, Lewis's granddaughter, etched into my mind the connection of Lewis with the gifted Harriet Beecher Stowe. My mother's readings of excerpts from *The Key to Uncle Tom's Cabin* about Clarke's experiences being the foundation for the character George Harris in the *Key* made me realize, at an early age, that Clarke was an extraordinary man. Knowing that about him was like having a family heirloom that made me feel proud, but I was hesitant to share the knowledge with anyone. I was in possession of my private treasure. What a gift my mother gave me.

Without the coincidental reconnection of my mother's favorite Aunt Minnie, Lewis's daughter, through Minnie's son Raymond Davis, nearly twenty-five years after Minnie's death, I would not have been able to write this book. Davis was the first person to reveal to our Seattle family the 1846 *Narratives* of Lewis and his brother Milton. This revelation made me appreciate for the first time that Clarke was truly a national public figure. Davis' information, however, did not pique my interest to the level of wanting to write a book exclusively on his life. Nevertheless, cousin Raymond certainly lit a spark in my mind that never died out.

I will always be indebted to my friend and colleague Professor C. Peter Ripley for providing me with information that gave academic legitimacy to the historic contributions of Lewis Clarke. His research contributions regarding *The Frederick Douglass Papers* under the leadership of the esteemed Professor John Blassingame of Yale University as well as Peter's *The Black Abolitionist Papers* revealed several more dimensions to the life and character of Clarke. Peter provided such an abundance of manuscripts, minutes, articles, etc., about Clarke that was like discovering the mother lode. Beyond what he did for me regarding my great-grandfather, Peter and his wife made my stay in Tallahassee some of the most memorable and enjoyable years I have ever experienced.

Gregory Wilson, Director of the Sugargrove, Pennsylvania Historical Society, read information about my connection with Lewis Clarke on the Internet in January 2005. He verified information I had about Clarke's years in Sugargrove and Busti, New York, across the Pennsylvania border. Greg also indicated that Clarke is still regarded as a hero in the section of the country. Just as important, he sent me an 1890 article from the *Washington Post* of an interview with Clarke. In it he said he was working on a manuscript about his entire life. There is no available information that it was completed. That statement by Lewis gave me the impetus to fulfill his dream through this publication. Thank you, Greg.

Special note must be made of my editor, Laura Kalpakian. Laura's in-depth analysis, corrections, and suggestions rescued my manuscript. Her hard-hitting, honest approach to editing has made me a better writer. Her periodic notes of encouragement gave me added fortitude to complete this project.

One of the most fulfilling aspects of working on this story has been reconnecting with my daughter Cynthia Marie Gayton, J.D., an adjunct professor in the Graduate School of Engineering at George Washington University. She has been a primary source for articles, books, manuscripts, photographs, etc., regarding Clarke for the past two years. Long, almost daily discussions of the phone with her have helped me crystallize ideas and approaches regarding the story. I cannot perceive of a better sounding board for this project. Obviously the connection goes beyond the professional issues relevant to the project. I have come to appreciate, to a greater degree, not only her brilliance but her sensitivity, compassion, and thoughtfulness.

I would not have been able to devote the time and energy on this book without the understanding and support of my wife, Carmen. We missed vacations or cut them short to allow me to meet real or perceived deadlines for the publication. Additionally, from time to time, her personal projects that could have benefitted from involvement were put on hold to allow me to work on the manuscript. Nevertheless she always encouraged me to keep moving forward toward the completion of the book. Thank you, love.

Notes

1. Carver Clark Gayton, "A Re-Introduction to Lewis Clarke, Harriet Beecher Stowe's Forgotten Hero," in Lewis Clarke's *Narrative of the Sufferings of Lewis Clarke: During Captivity of More Than Twenty-Five Years, among the Algerines of Kentucky, One of the So-Called Christian States of North America* (Seattle and London: University of Washington Press, 2012) vii.
2. Ibid.
3. Ibid.
4. Charles T. Davis and Henry Louis Gates, eds., *The Slave's Narrative* (Oxford and New York: Oxford University Press, 1985) xxi-xxii.
5. Ibid.
6. Ibid., xviii.
7. Yuval Taylor, ed., foreword by Charles Johnson, *I Was Born a Slave* (Chicago: Lawrence Hill Books, 1999) xvii.
8. Ibid., xxi.
9. John W. Blassingame, *The Slave Community: Plantation Life in the Antebellum South* (New York: Oxford University Press, 1972) 367.
10. Ibid., xxix-xxxi.
11. Ibid., xxvi.
12. "She was 'Little Eva,'" *Boston Daily Globe*, November 11, 1894, 29.
13. Ibid.
14. Bennett Young, *A History of Jassamine County* (Kentucky, Louisville, 1898) 95. Although Mrs. Banton makes reference to the War of 1812, she more than likely was generalizing the military requirements to which free white males ages 16-45 of Kentucky were liable. The 1792 Commonwealth Constitution of Kentucky, faced with Indian attacks and "situations of the country," established a statewide militia. The men were in the militia required to muster, i.e., convene, at least once a year for military maneuvers and, oftentimes, actual battles. They were

called the Cornstalk Militia because they usually could not afford weapons and used cornstalks for guns. The militia was also utilized during the War of 1812. Like Samuel Campbell, many in the militia were veterans of the Revolutionary War.

15. "She was Little Eva."

16. *Massachusetts Soldiers and Sailors in the Revolutionary War*, vol. 3, Secretary of the Commonwealth (Boston, MA: Wright Potter Printing, 1896-1908) 516, 538, 541, 591 and 595.

17. Lewis G. Clarke, *Narrative of the Sufferings of Lewis Clarke: During a Captivity of More Than Twenty-Five Years, among the Algerines of Kentucky, One of the So-Called Christian States of North America, Dictated by Himself* (Boston: David H. Ela, 1845) 9.

18. Alasdair Pettinger, "Frederick Douglass, Scotland and the South," *STAR* (*Scotland's Transatlantic Relations*) *Project Archive* (April 2004). Alasdair Pettinger of Scotland's Transatlantic Relations Project Archive commented that many African Americans must be counted as being of Scottish ancestry. "One striking example is that of Lewis Clarke." He pointed out that three of his grandparents were of Scots descent and that his father and grandfather fought "courageously" in the Revolutionary War. Pettinger goes on to say that Clarke was the model for George Harris in *Uncle Tom's Cabin*, "but he is not mentioned anywhere in Duncan A. Bruce's bestselling *The Mark of the Scots*, a book which lists famous people of Scots ancestry . . . which demonstrates 'their astonishing contributions to history, science, democracy, literature and the arts.'" He is surprised that General Colin Powell is the only African American listed in Bruce's book and Clarke is not. Pettinger places Clarke on this high pedestal without mentioning his considerable achievements beyond his connection with *Uncle Tom's Cabin*. The point here is that if a prominent Scottish academic can recognize the significant achievements of Clarke, maybe we in America should look more seriously into the life of one of our forgotten heroes. Hopefully this book will contribute toward that aspiration.

19. National Society of the Sons of the American Revolution, National Number 177314 (2011).

20. Lewis and Milton Clarke, *Narratives of the Sufferings of Lewis and Milton Clarke: Sons of a Soldier of the Revolution During Captivity of More Than Twenty-Five Years among the Slaveholders of Kentucky, One of the So-Called Christian States of North America* (Boston: Bela Marsh, 1846) 69-70.

21. *Court for Madison County, Kentucky: Banton and Wife against Campbell's Heirs*, &c. Fall Term (1834).

22. Lewis Clarke, *Narrative of the Sufferings of Lewis Clarke* (Boston, 1845) 8-11.

23. Ibid., 112

24. Ibid.

25. Ibid., 122

26. Lydia Maria Child, "Leaves from a Slave's Journal of Life," *New York Anti-Slavery Standard* (October 20 and 27, 1842).

27. Clarke, *Narrative of the Sufferings of Lewis Clarke*, 83.

28. Young E. Allison, "*Uncle Tom's Cabin's* Lewis Clarke, the George Harris of the Novel, Returns to the Old Farm . . . How Uncle Tom's Cabin Was Written and Incidents of George Harris's Life," *Louisville Courier*, May 16, 188,1.

29. Clarke, *Narrative of the Sufferings of Lewis Clarke*, 24.

30. Ibid., 28.

31. James Allison, "The Historical Background of Harriett Beecher Stowe's *Uncle Tom's Cabin*," *The Journal: Evansville Indiana* (April 15, 1881, 8-10). Clarke's contention that General Kennedy beat the slave Sam to death was not farfetched. Even slaveholders considered more "kindly" than most seldom strayed from the unwritten rules of the relationship between slave and slave master. Slaves had to always understand "their place." This fundamental evil of slavery was related in Stephen E. Ambrose's *Undaunted Courage,* the story of the Meriwether Lewis, and Captain Lewis Clark's exploration of the Louisiana Purchase Territory. York, the black slave of Clark's from childhood, assisted him during the arduous trek and "had help pole Clark's keelboat, paddled his canoe, hunted for his meat, made his fire, had shown he was prepared to sacrifice his life to save Clark's, crossed the continent and returned with his childhood companion, only to be beaten because he was insolent and sulky and denied not only his freedom but his wife and we may suppose, children." York had the "audacity" to ask for his freedom after they returned from the expedition [Stephen E. Ambrose, *Undaunted Courage, Meriwether Lewis, Thomas Jefferson, and the Opening of the American West* (New York, 1996) 448.]

32. Clarke, *Narrative of the Sufferings of Lewis Clark,* 65-68.

33. Ibid.

34. Ibid.

35. Lewis and Milton Clarke, *Narratives,* 82-97.

36. Ibid.

37. Lewis Clarke, *Narrative,* 32.

38. Ibid.

39. Ibid.

40. Ibid., 33.

41. Ibid., 35.

42. Ibid., 37.

43. Lewis and Milton Clarke, *Narrative of the Sufferings of Lewis and Milton Clarke*, 38.

44. Ibid., 38.

45. Ibid., 39.

46. Ibid., 41.

47. Ibid., 38.

48. James Allison (April 15, 1881) 1-17.

49. Ibid.

50. *Stevens Point Wisconsin Journal* (August 21, 1896).

51. "Uncle Tom's Cabin," *The Chicago Tribune* (August 30, 1880).

52. James Allison (April 15, 1881) 1-17.

53. Ibid., 44-45.

54. W. P. Fuller, "The Original George Harris," *New York Herald Tribune* (July 22, 1870).

55. W. P. Fuller, "A Figure in History: The Career of the Late Lewis Clarke," *Detroit Free Press* (February 19, 1898) 4.

56. Lewis Clarke, *Narrative*, 47-48.

57. Lewis Clarke, *Narrative*, 48-54.

58. Ibid.

59. Ibid.

60. Ibid.

61. Ibid.

62. Ibid., 55-56.

63. Franklin, *The Philanthropist* (Cincinnati, October 22, 1842).

64. Doris Kearns Goodwin, *Team of Rivals: The Political Genius of Abraham Lincoln* (New York: Simon & Schuster, 2005) 113. "Chase volunteered his services in many such cases. The eloquent power of his arguments soon earned him the honorary title of 'Attorney General for the Negro.'"

65. Lewis and Milton Clarke, *Narrative*, 92-95.

66. Lewis Clarke, *Narrative*, 58-60.

67. Joan D. Hedrick, *Harriet Beecher Stowe: a Life* (New York: Oxford University Press, 1994) 105-107.

68. Young Allison, 4.

69. James Brewer Stewart, *Holy Warriors* (New York: Hill and Hill, 1996) 54.

70. Ibid., 51-52.

71. Bertram Wyatt-Brown, *Lewis Tappan and the Evangelical War Against Slavery* (Baton Rouge and London: Louisiana State University Press, 1997) 108-109.

72. Ibid., 127.

73. Ibid., 130.

74. Ibid., 132.

75. Ibid., 187.

76. *The Liberator* (Boston: August 18, 1837).

77. Bertram Wyatt-Brown, 190.

78. Ibid.

79. Ibid., 197.

80. Ibid., 279-290.

81. *The Anti-Slave Standard* (New York, October 20 and 27, 1842).

82. Christine B. Hickman, "The Devil and the One Drop Rule: Racial Categories, African Americans, and the U. S. Census," *Michigan Law Review* (March 1997) 1-75.

83. Ibid.

84. Jane Ann and Bill Moore, Co-Directors of the Lovejoy Society, "Owen Lovejoy Website Message" (October 7, 2010).

85. Lewis Clarke, *Narrative,* vi.

86. Y. Allison, 3.

87. John W. Blassingame, et al., eds., Introduction, *Narrative of the Life of Frederick Douglass* (New Haven: Yale University Press, 2001) ix-xxxix.

88 ."Story of a Slave," *The Dubuque Herald* (December 21, 1901).

89. John W. Blassingame, Introduction, *Narrative of the Life of Frederick Douglas,* xxxviii.

90. Jane Ann and Bill Moore, Co-Directors, The Lovejoy Society Website (October 10, 2010).

91. William S. McFeely, *Frederick Douglass* (New York: Simon and Schuster, 1991) 158.

92. Henry Mayer, *All on Fire* (New York: W. W. Norton and Company, 1995) 431.

93. James Brewer Stewart, *Holy Warriors, the Abolitionists and American Slavery* (New York: Hill and Wang, 1997) 63.

94. John Stauffer, *The Black Hearts of Men: Radical Abolitionists and the Transformation of Race* (Cambridge and London: Harvard University Press, 2002) 68.

95. Y. Allison, 4.

96. Ibid.

97 Annie Fields, editor, *Life and Letters of Harriet Beecher Stowe* (Boston and New York, 1898) 84-85. Several respected biographers of Harriet Beecher Stowe contend that she first became interested in writing her novel resulted from a visit to Washington (Maysville) Kentucky in 1833 with her friend and teaching colleague from the Western Female Institute in Cincinnati, Mary Dutton. However, her nonchalant demeanor toward the slavery issue was also detected by

her friend. "Harriet did not seem to notice anything in particular that happened [regarding the slave culture] but sat much of the time as though abstracted in thought...the great subject of slavery was not yet the ruling thought of her existence." It is also interesting to note that Washington was on the same road of Lewis Clarke's 1841 escape route.

98. Claire Parfait, "The Publishing History of *Uncle Tom's Cabin*, 1852-2002" (Paris, France: Ashgate Publishing, Ltd., 2007) 16.

99. Bertram Wyatt-Brown, *Lewis Tappan and the Evangelical War Against Slavery*, 278-279. "Tappan began his most important contribution to political anti-slavery, the founding of the Washington *National Era*. Under the editorship of Gamaliel Bailey, Tappan's first choice for the position, the paper served effectively as the Liberty party's most popular journal. As usual, Tappan organized the fundraising for Bailey's salary and the paper's operation until it was self-supporting. He depended largely on old friends of the American and Foreign Anti-Slavery Society on both sides of the Atlantic who responded well. When the first issue appeared in January, 1847, Tappan was pleased with its neat appearance and moderate tone." The influence of Tappan's moderate mind set on the tenor of Stowe's *Uncle Tom's Cabin* is indicated in one of his editorials in the *Era*: "Candid men, in slave States, as well as the free States," he predicted, "will learn to distinguish between furious denunciators and those who aim to promote the true welfare . . . of both master and slave."

100. Y. Allison, 4.

101. Ibid.

102. Ibid.

103. Samuel Morison, Henry Commager, and William Leuchtenburg, *The Growth of the American Republic* (New York: Oxford University Press, 1980) 501-505.

104. Bertram Wyatt-Brown, *Lewis Tappan and the Evangelical War Against Slavery* (Baton Rouge, LA: Louisiana State University Press, 1969) 212.

105. "Once Famous Slave," *The Washington Post*.

106. Y. Allison, 6.

107. Michael Winship, '*Uncle Tom's Cabin,*' *History of the Book in the 19th Century United States, Uncle Tom's Cabin* in the Web of Culture Conference, University of Virginia, June 2007.

108. Hedrick, *Harriet Beecher Stowe: A Life*, 233.

109. Harriet Beecher Stowe, *The Key to Uncle Tom's Cabin* (London: Tomas Bosworth, 1853) 1-34.

110. Ibid.

111. Joan Hedrick, 211.

112. D. T. Baxter, "'Uncle George,' The Prototype of 'George Harris' in the Story of

Uncle Tom's Cabin Indulges in Some Reminiscences of Harriet Beecher Stowe," *Lexington, Kentucky Herald* (July 5, 1896) 3.

113. *The Times* (Richmond, VA, January 19, 1896) 4

114. Stanley Crouch and Playthell Benjamin, *Reconsidering the Souls of Black Folk* (Philadelphia-London: Running Press, 2002) 234-235. Stanley Crouch and Playthell Benjamin elaborate on Clarke's point: "After all, let us not forget *Uncle Tom's Cabin*, with its enormous sales and all of the discussion that it inspired, turned the nation against slavery and did more to bring on the war than all of the abolition talk and all the great Douglass had done."

115. D. T. Baxter, "'Uncle George: The Prototype of 'George Harris' in the Story of *Uncle Tom's Cabin*," 3.

116. Ibid.

117. Robert T. Treamoh, "The Half Not Told."

118. Frederick Douglass, *Life and Times of Frederick Douglass, Written by Himself* (Hartford, Connecticut, 1881) 289.

119. Frederick Douglass, 291-296.

120. Hedrick, 247.

121. Frederick Douglass, 296.

122. Hedrick, 248.

123. Ibid., 249.

124. Ibid.

125. Betty Fladeland, *Men and Brothers, Anglo-American Anti-Slavery Co-operation* (Urbana, Illinois, 1972) 357.

126. Hedrick, 240-248.

127. George M. Fredrickson, *The Black Image in the White Mind* (Middletown, Connecticut: Wesleyan University Press, 1987) 107-117.

128. Ibid., 22.

129. Claire Parfait, 16.

130. Child, "Leaves from a Slave's Journal of Life," *Anti-Slavery Standard* (October 20 and 27, 1842).

131. *The National Anti-Slavery Standard* (March 29, 1843).

132. Austin Willey, *The History of the Anti-Slavery Cause in State and Nation* (Portland Maine, 1886) 208-211.

133. Henry Bibb, "Communications from Henry Bibb," *The Signal of Liberty* (Sandwich, Ontario, Canada, August 21, 1847).

134. John Blassingame, xxii.

135. Ibid., 103.

136. W. P. Fuller, "Uncle Tom's Cabin: The Original George Harris."

137. *North Star* (Buffalo, New York, January 7, 1848).

138. "Tale of Gerrit Smith Behind Adirondack Suit," *The New York Times* (November 19, 1904).

139. *North Star* (Rochester, New York, August 11, 1848).

140. "Colored Man in the Cambridge Common Council," *The Boston Globe* (April 17, 1901).

141. Stowe, *Key to Uncle Tom's Cabin*, 29. Because of Lewis's complexion, Northern audiences were wary of Lewis's authenticity despite Harriet Beecher Stowe's accurate observation that "the case of Lewis Clarke's [experience as a slave] is a harder one than common [within slavery]. The case of Douglass is probably a very fair average specimen."

142. "Old and Poor: Lewis G. Clarke of 'Uncle Tom's Cabin.' He Was the 'George Harris' of Famous Story. Real Facts Which He Gave to Mrs. Stowe, Told for the First Time in the Globe, Brother Lives in Cambridge and Wants Him to Come Here," *The Boston Globe* (November 29, 1895).

143. "Dr. S. L. Fraser Dead, Aged 83," *Post-Standard* (June 14, 1933).

144. Roy L. Blodgett, letter, Underground Railroad in Chautauqua County, New York and Warren County, Pennsylvania (1944) 22-25.

145. "Uncle Tom's Cabin," *The Chicago Tribune* (August 30, 1880).

146. Roy L. Blodgett, letter.

147. "Interesting Letter—The Fugitive Slave Harrison," *Frederick Douglass Papers* (November 6, 1851).

148. "Underground Railroad," *Town of Busti, History* website.

149. Stowe, *Uncle Tom's Cabin*, 116.

150. David Levering Lewis, W. E. B. Dubois, *Biography of a Race* (New York: Henry Holt & Company, 1993) 45.

151. "Call for a North American Convention," *Voice of the Fugitive* (August 27, 1851).

152. Peter Ripley, ed., *The Black Abolitionist Papers*, vol. II (Canada 1830-1865, Chapel Hill: University of North Carolina Press, 1986) 270-278.

153. Ibid.

154. W. P. Fuller, *Uncle Tom's Cabin: The Original George Harris*.
    Clarke, among others, discussed attacking Harper's Ferry, Virginia, with John Brown in Essex County, New York, in the late 1840s; however, the scheme was rejected as impractical. The fervor against slavery reached a higher level in the North by the late 1850s. John Brown convened another council of war in Detroit, which Clarke attended in May of 1858 while he was living in East Sandwich, Ontario, Canada. The meeting adjourned to Chatham, Ontario, located across the border from Detroit. Clarke took part in the deliberations and predicted disaster. He refused to become involved with Brown's proposed attacks on Harper's Ferry. Clarke told Brown that his efforts to accommodate

escaping slaves into Canada fully occupied his time. Brown, on October 16, 1859, led an armed unit of black and white men who attacked and occupied the Federal arsenal at Harper's Ferry, Virginia, and was subsequently captured and executed. He was buried in New York at his home in North Elba, Essex County, New York, where years before Clarke was offered property by Brown ally and philanthropist Gerrit Smith.

155. "Minutes from the General Convention," (Amherstburg, Ontario, Canada, June 10 and 17, 1853).

156. Franklin Richard Miller, personal diary, Warren County Historical Society (February 2, 1854).

157. "Letter from the Editor, Sherman, Chautauqua County, New York," *North Star* (Rochester, New York, June 23, 1854).

158. "Pageant Tops Celebration of GOP's 100th Anniversary," *Waterloo Daily Courier* (July 4, 1954).

159. Ibid.

160. Jackson Scrapbook, Jackson Public Library (Jackson, Michigan, April 11, 1965).

161. William Stocking, ed., "Under the Oaks," *Detroit Tribune* (1904).

162. August Lightfoot, "Meeting of Colored Citizens at the City Hall," *The Frederick Douglass Papers, vol. 2* (Rochester, New York, August 31, 1855).

163. Morison, Commager, and Leuchtenburg, 586-587.

164. Ibid.

165. Ibid.

166. Doris K. Goodwin, *Team of Rivals,* 184-185.

167. "Radical Abolition Meeting," *Warren Mail* (Sugar Grove, PA, Thursday, August 9, 1856) c. 5, p. 2.

168. Morison, Commager, and Leuchtenburg, 593-595.

169. Ibid.

170. Minutes of the Agricultural, Mechanical, and Educational Association of Canada West Convention (Sandwich, Ontario, Canada, March 1, 1859).

171. "Colored People in Council," *New York Times* (August 3, 1859).

172. Ibid.

173. C. Peter Ripley, ed., *The Black Abolitionist Papers, Volume II,* 270.

174. "'George Harris': The Historic Character of Mrs. Stowe's Immortal Story," *Detroit Free Press* (June 10, 1885).

175. Ibid.

176. W. P. Fuller, *New York Herald Tribune,* July 22, 1870.

177. *The Washington Post* (May 12, 1890). Clarke often mentioned that his wife "was a directed descendent of the renowned Randolph family, of Virginia." Research continues to take place to verify his assertion.

178. Josiah Henson with John Lobb, *Autobiography of Josiah Henson* (Boston, 1879).

179. W. P. Fuller, "Uncle Tom's Cabin" (July 22, 1870).

180. Michael Gladstone White, "The Promised Land? Windsor's City Hall Square-Terminus of the Underground Railroad," *Walkerville Times* (2013).

181. William Bigglestone, *They Stopped in Oberlin: Black Residents and Visitors of the Nineteenth Century* (Oberlin Ohio: Oberlin College, 2002) 43-47.

182. "Uncle Tom's Cabin," *The Chicago Tribune* (August 30, 1880).

183. US Federal Census (1980).

184. "Daughter of 'George Harris' of 'Uncle Tom' Fame, Living in the City," *The Freeman's Newspaper* (April 4, 1891).

185. *The History of the Anti-Slavery Cause in State and Nation* (Portland, Maine, 1886) 211-212.

186. "The Old Fugitive Slaves," *Colorado Springs Gazette* (May 20, 1876).

187. John Hope Franklin, *From Slavery to Freedom, a History of Negro Americans, Third Edition* (New York: Alfred A. Knopf, 1969) 335-338.

188. Ibid.

189. The life of escaped slave Josiah Henson was used as one of the models of the character Uncle Tom in Stowe's book. Clarke and Henson knew each other for years in Kentucky as well as Canada. Clarke told of Henson in his conversations with Stowe at the home of her in-laws, the Saffords in Cambridge during the early and middle 1840s. Although Stowe briefly referred to Henson's 1849 narrative in the *Key,* she did not meet him until after the 1852 publication of her novel. Henson's several narratives, as a result of the publication of *Uncle Tom's Cabin,* were very popular and were translated worldwide. Historians also agree, however, that despite his later fame as the original Uncle Tom, his life had little relationship to the saintly title character or the popular stereotype that followed. His narrative reflects that he suffered little ill treatment at the hands of owners and never admits to having been whipped or severely punished. Historians have described him as intelligent, vain, manipulative, "a specialist at charlatanry" and an "insufferable egotist." No such epithets were hurled at Clarke during his lifetime.

190. "Lewis George Clarke," *Stevens Point [Wisconsin] Journal* (August 21, 1896). "Uncle Tom's Cabin," *Louisville Courier* (May 16, 1881).

191. Montgomery, *"Uncle Tom's Cabin,* An Interview with Lewis Clarke, the 'George Harris' of the Story, The Narrative of His Life—His Escape from Kentucky to Canada in 1841," *The Chicago Tribune* (August 30, 1880).

192. "She Was 'Little Eva,'" *The Boston Globe* (November 11, 1894).

193. "Finished: The Life of George Lewis Clark Comes to an End," *Lexington Herald* (December 17, 1897) 1.

194. *The National Republican* (Washington, DC, June 4, 1883).

195. Benjamin Brawley, *Negro Builders and Heroes* (Chapel Hill: University of North Carolina Press, 1937) 144-146.

196. Daniel J. Sharfstein, *The Invisible Line* (New York: The Penguin Press, 2011) 197-212.

197. *Journal of Social Science* (Boston, May 1880) XI, 35.

198. Benjamin Brawley, 143.

199. *New York Times* (September 13, 1879).

200. Daniel J. Sharfstein, 198.

201. "Uncle Tom's Cabin," *The Chicago Tribune* (August 30, 1880).

202. *The Lexington Leader* (February 1, 1891) 5.

203. "Once a Famous Slave," *Washington Post* (May 12, 1890).

204. Ibid.

205. "*Uncle Tom's Cabin*: Something about the Real Hero of the Famous Book," *Monticello [Iowa] Express* (July 9, 1891).

206. "Uncle Tom's Cabin," *The Chicago Tribune* (August 30, 1880).

207. "Once a Famous Slave," *The Washington Post* (May 12, 1890).

208. Robert T. Teamoh, "The Half Not Told," *The Boston Globe* (May 20, 1891).

209. "Rejoice in Their Freedom: Reminiscences of the Slave Days of Harriet Beecher Stowe's 'George Harris,'" *The Boston Globe* (May 19, 1891).

210. "Honored: For the Part He Played in Making History," *The Lexington Daily Leader* (December 19, 1897).

211. Ibid.

212. "Pitiful is the Condition of Lewis George Clarke, the Original Uncle Tom of Harriet Beecher Stowe's 'Uncle Tom's Cabin,'" *The Press-Transcript* (Lexington, Kentucky, Saturday, November 23, 1895).

213. "Not 'Uncle Tom,'" *The Evening Bulletin* (Maysville, Kentucky, December 9, 1895) 3.

214. Robert Teamoh, "The Half Not Told" (May 20, 1891).

215. Stowe, *Key to Uncle Tom's Cabin*, 34.
    David S. Reynolds, *Mightier Than the Sword* (New York and London: W. W. Norton and Company, 2011) 87.

216. "Mrs. H. B. Stowe vs. Lewis Clark," *Boston Transcript* (December 4, 1895).

217. Hedrick, 397.

218. Hedrick, 397-398.

219. "Mrs. H. B. Stowe Never Saw Clark. The World Promoting His False Pretense That He Is George Harris," *New York Sun* (December 6, 1895).

220. "The Press: The King is Dead," *Time* (August 20, 1951).

221. *The Sun* (New York, December 10, 1895) 7.

222. "A Parallel for Mrs. Stowe," *The Times* (Richmond, Kentucky, January 19, 1896) 4.

223. Ibid.

224. Ibid.

225. Ibid.

226. Jacques B. Vest, "Making Authenticity: Polk Miller and the Evolution of American Popular Culture," MA thesis, Virginia Commonwealth University (2008).

227. "End Is Near: 'George Harris' Soon to Face the Last Great Master," *Lexington Daily Leader* (December 2, 1895).

228. "Lewis George Clarke Overcome by Heat," *The Climax* (Richmond, Kentucky, August 12, 1896) 4.

229. "End Is Near: 'George Harris' Soon to Face the Last Great Master," *Lexington Daily Leader* (December 2, 1895).

230. "A Benefit Entertainment," *Otago Witness* (Dunedin, New Zealand, October 8, 1896) 39.

231. Ibid.

232. "FINISHED: The Life of George Lewis Clarke Comes to a Close with Evening," *Lexington Morning Herald* (December 17, 1897) 1.

233. *The Herald* (Lexington, Kentucky, January 7, 1897).

234. "FINISHED: The Life of George Lewis Clarke Comes to Close with Evening," *The Lexington Herald* (December 17, 1897) 1.

235. Ibid.

236. "HONORED: For the Part He Played in Making History," *The Lexington Daily Reader* (December 19, 1897).

237. "Uncle Tom's Cabin: Death of the Original of George Harris," *Otago Witness* (Dunedin, New Zealand, February 10, 1898).

238. "Once a Famous Slave," *Washington Post* (May 12, 1890).

239. "Daughter of George Harris of 'Uncle Tom' Fame Living in the City," *The Freeman Newspaper* (Indianapolis, April 4, 1891).

240. *The Southern News* (Richmond, VA, October 15, 1892) 1.

241. "Death of a Noted Character: John Milton Clarke Said to Have Been a White Slave—Served in the Civil War," *Cambridge Chronicle* (March 2, 1901).

242. "Old and Poor, Lewis Clarke of 'Uncle Tom's Cabin,'" *The Boston Globe* (November 29, 1895).

243. "Clark's Family Affairs," *Boston Journal* (December 20, 1897).

244. "Dying Man Warns Boston Editors: Tells Them Not to Print Stories of His Early Life When He Is Dead," *Boston Globe* (December 1, 1900).

245. Daniel Murray, "John Milton Clarke," Manuscript Division, US Library of Congress (Washington, DC, January 16, 1901).

246. Henry E. Baker, "A Memorial to a Devoted Wife Violetta Clark Baker" (Washington, DC, 1923).

247. "Story of a Slave: J. Milton Clarke Says He Inspired *Uncle Tom's Cabin*," *New York Sun* (December 21, 1900).

248. "Rejoice in Their Freedom," *Boston Daily Globe* (May 18, 1891).

249. "Left $5 Each, Two Sons of J. Milton Clarke Contest Will," *The Boston Globe* (March 29, 1901).

250. Tyrone Beason, "We Have a Unique Story to Tell," *Seattle Times* (January 16, 2005), 1.

251. "Once a Famous Slave," *The Washington Post* (May 12, 1890).

252. Harriet Beecher Stowe, *Uncle Tom's Cabin,* with a new introduction by Charles Johnson (London, Oxford University Press, 2002) 21.

253. Ibid., 24.

254. Ibid., 4.

255. Ibid., 65.

256. Ibid., 366.

257. Ibid., 422.

258. Ibid., 440.

259. Ibid., 446.

260. Ibid., 447.

Bibliography (Selected)

Allen, William B., *Rethinking Uncle Tom: The Political Philosophy of Harriet Beecher Stowe.* Lanham, MD: Lexington Books, 2009.

Allison, James. "The Historical Background of Harriet Beecher Stowe's Uncle Tom's Cabin." Evansville (IN) Journal, April 15, 1881.

Allison, Young E. "Uncle Tom's Cabin's Lewis Clarke, the 'George Harris' of the Novel, Returns to the Old Farm." Louisville Courier, May 16, 1881.

Ambrose, Stephen E. Undaunted Courage. New York: Simon & Schuster, 1996.

Applegate, Debbie. The Most Famous Man in America: The Biography of Henry Ward Beecher. New York: Doubleday, 2006.

Baldwin, James. Baldwin: Collected Essays. New York: The Library of America, 1998.

Barker, Joseph. The Lives of Lewis, Milton and Cyrus Clarke: Three Celebrated Fugitive Slaves. London: Wortley, 1846.

Barker, Joseph. Interesting Memoirs & Documents Relating to American Slavery. London: Chapman Brothers, 1846

Beason, Tyrone. "We Have a Unique Story to Tell." Seattle Times, January 16, 2005.

Bigglestone, William. They Stopped in Oberlin. Oberlin, Ohio: Oberlin College, 2002.

Brawley, Benjamin. Negro Builders and Heroes. Chapel Hill, NC: University of North Carolina Press, 1937.

Child, Lydia Maria. "Leaves from a Slave's Journal of Life." New York Anti-Slavery Standard. October 20 and 27, 1842.

Clarke, Lewis Garrard. Narrative of the Sufferings of Lewis Clarke: During Captivity of More Than Twenty-Five Years among the Algerines of Kentucky, One of the So-Called Christian States of North America. Boston: David H. Ela, 1845.

Clarke, Lewis, and Milton Clarke. Narratives of the Sufferings of Lewis and Milton Clarke: Sons of a Soldier of the Revolution During Captivity of More Than Twenty-Five years among the Slaveholders of Kentucky, One of the So-Called Christian States of North America. Boston: Bela Marsh, 1846.

Coleman, J. W. Slavery Times in Kentucky. Chapel Hill, NC: University of North Carolina Press, 1940.

Cone, James H. Martin & Malcolm & America: A Dream or a Nightmare. Maryknoll, New York: Orbis Books, 1991.

Crouch, Stanley, and Playthell Benjamin. Reconsidering the Souls of Black Folk, Thoughts on the Groundbreaking Classic Work of W. E. B. DuBois. Philadelphia: Running Press, 2002.

Cruse, Harold. The Crisis of the Negro Intellectual, from Its Origins to the Present. New York: William Morrow & Company, Inc., 1967.

Culp, Daniel Wallace. Twentieth Century Negro Literature, or A Cyclopedia of Thought on the Vital Topics Relating to the American Negro, by One Hundred of America's Greatest Negroes. Toronto, Canada: J. L. Nichols & Co., 1902.

Davis, Charles T. and Gates, Henry Louis Jr., eds. The Slave's Narrative. Oxford: Oxford University Press, 1985.

De Lombard, Jeannine Marie. Slavery on Trial: Law, Abolitionism, and Print Culture. Chapel Hill, North Carolina: University of North Carolina Press, 2007.

Douglass, Frederick. Narrative of the Life of Frederick Douglass: American Slave. Edited by John Blassingame, John R. McKivign, and Peter P. Hinks. New Haven, CT: Yale University Press, 2001.

Du Bois, W. E. B. The Souls of Black Folk. With an introduction by John Edgar Wideman. New York: Vantage Books, 1990.

Franklin. "Captors Caught." The Philanthropist. Cincinnati, October 22, 1842.

Franklin, John Hope. From Slavery to Freedom: A History of Negro Americans. Third edition. New York: Alfred A. Knopf, 1966.

Fredrickson, George M. The Black Image in the White Mind: The Debate on Afro-American Character and Destiny, 1817-1914. Middletown, Connecticut: Wesleyan University Press, 1987.

Fuller, W. P. "A Figure in History, the Career of the Late Lewis Clarke." Detroit Free Press, February 19, 1898.

Fuller, W. P. "Uncle Tom's Cabin: The Original George Harris." New York Herald Tribune, July 22, 1870.

Goodwin, Doris Kearns. Team of Rivals: The Political Genius of Abraham Lincoln. New York: Simon & Schuster, 2005.

Gonzalez, Juan and Torres, Joseph. News for All the People: The Epic Story of Race and the American People. London and New York: Verso, 2011.

Gwathmey, John H. Historical Register of Virginia in the Revolution, 1775-1783. Quintin Publications Collection, Genealogical Publishing Company, Inc., 1979.

Hahn, Steven. The Political Worlds of Slavery and Freedom. Cambridge, Massachusetts, and London, England: Harvard University Press, 2009.

Hedrick, Joan D. Harriet Beecher Stowe: A Life. New York: Oxford University Press, 1994.

Hogan, Roseann Reinemuth. Kentucky Ancestry: A Guide to Genealogical and Historical Research. Provo, Utah: Ancestry Publishing, 1992.

Hoover, Dwight W., ed. Understanding Negro History. Chicago: Quadrangle Books, 1968.

Lewis, David Levering. W. E. B. Du Bois: Biography of a Race. New York: Henry Holt and Company, 1993.

"Lewis George Clarke, the Prototype of a Character in Uncle Tom's Cabin." Stevens Point (WI) Journal, August 21, 1896.

Lucas, Marion. A History of Blacks in Kentucky, Vol.1, From Slavery to Segregation, 1760-1891. The KentuckyHistorical Society, 1992.

Massachusetts Soldiers and Sailors of the Revolutionary War, Vols. 1-17. Secretary of the Commonwealth. Boston: Wright and Porter Printing, 1896-1908.

Mayer, Henry. All on Fire: William Lloyd Garrison and the Abolition of Slavery. New York and London: W. W. Norton & Company, 1998.

McCullough, David. 1776. New York: Simon and Schuster, 2005.

Morison, Samuel Eliot, and Henry Steele Commager. The Growth of the American Republic. New York: Oxford University Press, 1980.

"Not an Uncle Tom." Evening Bulletin. Maysville, Kentucky, December 9, 1895.

"Once a Famous Slave." Washington Post, May 12, 1890.

Report of the National Advisory Commission on Civil Disorders. Washington, DC :The Government Printing Office, 1968.

Reynolds, David S. Uncle Tom's Cabin and the Battle for America: Mightier Than the Sword. New York: W. W. Norton, 2011.

Ripley, C. Peter, et al. The Black Abolitionist Papers. Chapel Hill, North Carolina: University of North Carolina Press, 1985.

Sharfstein, Daniel J. Three American Families and the Secret Journey from Black to White: The Invisible Line. New York: The Penguin Press, 2011.

"She was Little Eva." Boston Daily Globe, November 11, 1894.

Stewart, James Brewer. Holy Warriors: The Abolitionists and American Slavery. New York: Hill and Wang, 1997.

Stowe, Harriet Beecher. The Annotated Uncle Tom's Cabin. Edited by Henry Lewis Gates Jr. and Hollis Robbins. New York: W. W. Norton and Company, 2007.

_____. Key to Uncle Tom's Cabin: The Original Facts and Documents Upon Which the Story Is Founded, Together with Corroborative Statements Verifying the Truth of the Work. London: Tomas Bosworth, 1853.

_____. Uncle Tom's Cabin. Introduction by Charles Johnson. Oxford and New York: Oxford University Press, 2002.

Taylor, Yuval, ed. I Was Born a Slave: An Anthology of Classic Slave Narratives. Vol. I: 1772-1849. Chicago: Lawrence Hill Books, 1999.

"Uncle Tom's Cabin: An Interview with Lewis Clarke, the 'George Harris' of the Story." Chicago Tribune, August 30, 1880.

Vacheenas, Jean, and Betty Volk. "Born in Bondage: History of a Slave Family." Negro History Bulletin, May 1973.

Wilkerson, Isabel. The Warmth of Other Suns: The Epic Story of America's Great Migration. New York: Random House, 2010.

Wyatt-Brown, Bertram. Lewis Tappan and the Evangelical War Against Slavery. Baton Rouge, Louisiana: Louisiana State University Press, 1969.

About the Author

The author, Carver Clark Gayton is the great-grandson of Clarke. He received his PhD in political science from the University of Washington. He served as Director of Affirmative Action Programs at the University of Washington, assistant professor of public administration at Florida State University, Corporate Director of Educational Relations and Training at The Boeing Company, lecturer at the University of Washington Evans School of Public Administration and Executive Director of the Northwest African American Museum. He lives in Seattle.